DEAR DOLPHIN -

Iskra's Atlantic Adventures

Frank Mulville

To Wendy

For to a prodigal, the joy of living
Is not in having for oneself but giving,
For life is emptiness and nature bare
Lacking the friend to have the larger share

John Masefield

Text and illustrations © Frank Mulville

First published in 1991 by Ashford, Buchan & Enright,
31 Bridge Street, Leatherhead, Surrey

ISBN PB 1 85253 244 0

Cover: *Iskra* off Cape Horn, the northern cape of Iceland. Water colour
by John Todds.

Line drawings by Walter Kemsley.
Maps by M. N. Downie.
Frontis by Jane Michaelis
Photographs by the author

Parts of this book have been published in *Yachting Monthly* and *Yachts and Yachting* magazines and in the American magazines *Sail* and *Cruising World*. The author would like to thank the editors for their permission to reprint.

A catalogue record for this book is available from the British Library.

Typeset by Priory Publications, Haywards Heath
Printed in Great Britain by FotoDirect Ltd., Brighton

Contents

I

Destiny

We came up with the island of Flores in the Azores at dusk, rounding the southern point as the light was fading. I remember it as a bluff 400 feet high, the lighthouse perched on a rock ledge, the precipitous slopes densely wooded, the island rising to a peak through green valleys, here and there a patchwork of closely cultivated fields and terraces, a halo of cloud round its peak. It looked threatening. If it had not been that precise time of day the events which changed the course of my life, perhaps all our lives, would not have taken place. As *Girl Stella* came round the point the lights of the little town of Santa Cruz began to sparkle in the soft evening air. It was calm in the lee of the island, the boat was suddenly still after weeks of movement, sheltered from the rough swells of the Atlantic Ocean, gliding silently along the shore, her sails catching whiffs and eddies of air that found their way over the mountains. We watched fascinated, standing silent on *Girl Stella's* ample decks: the two boys, Celia and Dick, sons, wife, friend and me at the wheel. As the light faded the island became black against the starlit sky, standing out of the sea like a clenched hand, risen from the deep to warn us. The warning fell on my closed ears.

Celia said, 'Not much doing here - we ought to keep right on, get on home; that's where we're going.'
Patrick said, 'It's crazy to go past this lovely place - a brand new island - and not go ashore. When will we ever be here again?'
Adrian said, 'We'll be late for school - and anyway, I want to see the dog.' Dick was non-committal - he always was. 'It's all the same to me,' he said, 'but it would be nice to see it.'

A skipper's job is to resolve conflict, to know what is to be done and to see to it that it is done; to listen to opinions, wishes, doubts and then to make his decision firmly and with no room for equivocation. I was a bad skipper on this day; I failed them because I took too much account of them, baulked at riding rough-shod over any of them. The dual tasks of skipper and father of a family do not ride easily together. I was pulled first one way and then another by Celia's and the boys' often conflicting and always powerful personalities working on me from opposite

1

directions. It always happened and I was powerless against it - I didn't understand it then, but I knew it was happening.

Celia's judgement was often right but it was based on instinct, not on knowledge. She was frightened of the sea but, being a brave person, she disguised her fear. It came out of her as nervousness and, after she had children, as lack of confidence. Her imagination raced on ahead of her, leading her children into dangers that did not yet exist. It wasn't that she showed the nervousness to the outside world, but it was there and I picked it up on the two-way communications system which operates between people who are close to one another. I was instinctively aware of her lack of confidence and so I was driven to go against her judgements even though I often knew they were sound. It was a kind of perversity that I was dimly aware of but couldn't explain or understand. Celia and I were in a partnership which carried with it all the ingredients of disaster. I loved my family; individually and in their separate ways they loved me; but taken together their effect on me was destructive.

'We'll hang on for the night,' I said. 'It's calm out here. We'll wait till morning, then when we can see we'll decide what to do.' At that moment the leading lights above the harbour of Santa Cruz were suddenly switched on - two powerful white beacons showing the way into the harbour. My own judgement switched off at the same moment.

Dick said, 'There, it looks like they're expecting us.' Patrick said, 'Hooray, now we can go in.' Celia went below. I said, 'All right, we'll go in'. Clearly *Girl Stella* had been seen approaching in the dusk and they had switched on the lights to help her in. It must be a good harbour. The Admiralty Pilot book mentioned it but gave no details. Flores was a whaling port, it was reasonable to suppose that the harbour was safe for a forty-foot yacht. If we had arrived in daylight I would have seen that the harbour of Santa Cruz, if it can be called a harbour, was unsuitable for a vessel of *Girl Stella's* size - or for any yacht. It was tiny, it was ridden with rocks and it had a surge which washed over the stone quay with destructive energy. I would have rejected the harbour, looked at the anchorage under the cliff and made my decision. If we had raised the island in the night there would have been no question of going in. The inhabitants would have been asleep and the lights would not have been switched on. As it was, there were a dozen men on the quay to take our lines. The last of the daylight still lingered in the sky, leaving behind a flat pallor. The men stood in a group, their boots washed by the swirling surf, shouting instructions at us. Flores is a remote place, a visitor is a rare bird, only to be encouraged.

As soon as *Girl Stella* was in the entrance I understood the folly of it. It was a trap. Black rocks flashed past close to port and to starboard. It was already too late to turn back. I believe I understood then that *Girl Stella* was in the grip of something she would never escape from; there was a certain inevitability, as if it was all planned, tied up, delivered. The surge had swept her in through the narrow cut - into a pool perhaps twenty yards across. 'Hard to starboard,' Dick shouted from the bow. 'Full astern.' I turned the wheel, slammed the engine into reverse, advanced the throttle. She pulled up juddering. Dick flung a heaving line; the waiting men pulled her alongside.

They were all shouting in Portuguese. *Girl Stella* was against her fenders, crashing into the stone face of the jetty, surging fore and aft, snatching at her lines. She banged her keel on the bottom, a crash that shook her as if she had been picked up and dropped. We moved her a few feet forward where it was deeper. 'We can't stay here, Dick, we'll have to get out.' A burly man stepped forward from the crowd. 'I Pilot' he said, in English; 'I take to Porto Piqueran - very safe place; you all right there.' He jumped aboard and took the wheel. 'Let go,' he shouted. 'Slow ahead, Captain. The pilot took *Girl Stella* out the way we had come in, manoeuvring and turning her as if he had known her all his life.

That crash lodged itself in my mind like a needle injecting me with fear. I knew *Girl Stella* was weak where she had struck the rock bottom. The others knew nothing of it but I knew - I had been carrying the knowledge with me, unshared with Celia or Dick or the boys, since *Girl Stella* had been in Castries in the West Indian island of St Lucia nearly six months earlier. There, she had been hauled out on the slip for painting. She had always leaked - not seriously but not inconsiderably, a little each day, quite a lot if she was left for a week unattended. It was a consistent leak; it would increase a little in bad weather but not dangerously. I had installed an electric pump as a precaution. We all knew about it - all old boats leak a bit, we said to ourselves. But we didn't know where the water came in. Whenever she had been on the slip we had searched her bottom for a leak but we had never discovered anything amiss with her. I found out in Castries.

She was hauled out on the slip, the others were off in the town; I was wandering around looking at the lovely wooden hull. The foreman of the yard came up to me - a delightful West Indian. 'You seen this sar?' he said. He took a crowbar and prised the iron band away from *Girl Stella's* keel; then he pushed his knife in. It disappeared to the hilt. A stream of water came out. One of the keel bolts had rotted away to nothing, the timber round it was soft. With a keen, practised eye for the old wooden schooners of the Caribbean the foreman had noticed a suspicious patch. With tact and consideration he had waited until everything was quiet before showing it to me. To replace the keel bolt would be a major job; the engine would have to come out, possibly a piece of timber scarfed into the keel itself. To have it done there in Castries would cost more money than we had, would take weeks, and he doubted whether they could do the job in the yard. The voyage to Cuba, which we were engaged in, would have to be abandoned.

I looked at him and he looked at me. It all raced through my mind: give up the voyage? get *Girl Stella* to a good yard? where? Leave her and go home? Impossible. I said, 'Get some gunge - we'll patch it up somehow.' He said, 'To sail across the ocean?' Sure, it'll be all right; it'll get her home - then we'll have a proper job done'. He went off and found a tin of some mastic compound - thick, sticky stuff. He worked it in with a putty knife, into the wet porous orifice that was in *Girl Stella's* keel - a festering sore in the heart of her. I went on board, brought down a sheet of lead, copper nails. We covered it with a neat patch, under her bottom and a few inches up either side of the keel, all nicely nailed in place. Then we put the keel band back, hammered it home, touched up the paint. It worked - she hardly leaked from then on. Now, six months on, in Flores of the Azores, I knew she had injured herself exactly on that patch. I knew that she was damaged.

The pilot took *Girl Stella* towards the north of the island. 'Porto Piqueran - whaling factory.' he said. The island was a black shape towering up beside us, the lights of farms and villages glittering to match the sky above with its million stars. Round the shore where the swell growled over the rocks we could see the sudden flashes of the surf. Then the pilot turned *Girl Stella* towards the shore, as if to crash her against the cliff's face - no leading lights

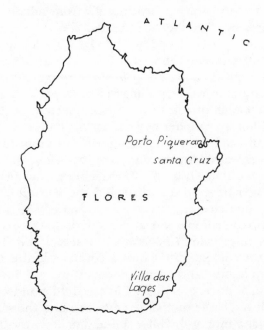

here, only a wall of black rock and, below, the silver flashes strewn around like tinsel. 'No worry,' he said, sensing my alarm, 'You safe here - I know the way.' He spun the wheel and we turned hard to port, close under the shore, inside the rocks; there was a channel, winding and twisting itself back towards the south. Suddenly the shore opened out to starboard and we were in a narrow cleft, a wedge cut out of the island like a slice of cake. Ahead the rock closed tight shut, high walls on each side, the sky a dark triangle above our heads, a stone jetty to starboard, the sea behind us all studded with rock, the surf gently breaking. The pilot and his helpers jumped into *Girl Stella's* dinghy and ran out ropes to the rocks. They tied her in a cat's cradle to both sides of the cleft, like a spider in the centre of her web.

It was calm in Porto Piqueran, the swell dead, the clouds above us marching across the sky towards England. The pilot and his companions came down to the cabin and drank stiff tots of Cuban rum. It warmed them and loosened their tongues. 'Castro an anti-Christ?' the pilot shouted. 'And the people pay no rent? Ha! - here the landlord is an aristocrat - he lives in Portugal, has never seen Flores'. They went ashore late. I ferried them to the stone steps and they marched off up the long ramp that leads to the whaling factory, swaying rhythmically from side to side. 'We see you tomorrow. Sleep well. You safe here.'

The boys went to sleep first, then Dick, then Celia. I lay awake. Through the skylight above my head I could see the top of the cliff, beyond it sky and stars. *Girl Stella* was moving softly fore and aft and from side to side, pulling first on one rope then on another as if to test each one in turn, to gauge their strength. The pilot had tied her up with her bow in, her stern towards the entrance. He had insisted on this. 'Strong wind from west here', he had said, 'bow towards strong wind, best ropes for'ard.' 'Suppose we want to get out in a hurry?' 'You safe here, wind always from west - no danger here.' I had shrugged and let him have his way. I counted their sleeping breaths and then got up - through the saloon, up the companion ladder and on to the deck.

It was quiet, calm; *Girl Stella* was peaceful. I walked along the deck to the cockpit, lifted a brass cover set in the deck, grasped the pump handle and began to work it up and down. It caught its suction at once; every time I lowered it I could hear the water gurgle through the discharge and drop into the sea. While the engine was running the bilge was always kept dry; the pump was connected to it and ran automatically with it. The engine had been stopped for three hours. She would have made a drop - perhaps seven or eight strokes. I pumped ten strokes. Then I pumped ten more - then ten more strokes, counting, counting. I felt myself go pale in the darkness. I felt a sick emptiness inside myself. At one hundred and fifty-three strokes the pump sucked air. Perhaps the engine pump hadn't been connected? I went below, down the engine room hatch, shone a torch - it was connected. There was no doubt. She had damaged herself, opened her old wound. She was leaking twenty times more than she had leaked before.

The next day was bright and warm. At eight there was a shout from the quay. A tall, sallow man with glassy eyes came on board. He wore a long green coat over a dirty uniform, his teeth were black, his breath smelt of last night's garlic. He and a companion searched the ship from bow to stern. I don't know what they were looking for - what they found were books. In Cuba everyone gave books, they were the currency of appreciation. Most of them were in Spanish, some in English, a few even in Portuguese. Most of them were tracts on one aspect or another of the Cubans' new philosophy. The Cubans, having just aspired to universal literacy,

6

regarded books with particular respect - they were the symbol of their enlightenment. The customs officer regarded them with the utmost suspicion.

I went ashore with him and he took me on a round of the officialdom of the island; customs, immigration, police, international police. Each body tried to take our passports but I steadfastly refused to part with them. 'We must have our passports', I said; 'We might want to leave the island in a hurry.' Having come from Cuba they believed that we were the spearhead of some fifth column prepared to spread dissent among the people of Flores. After much argument they gave permission for *Girl Stella* to stay in the island for a few days. I went back on board, brought the others ashore and we walked into the little town of Santa Cruz, looked at the harbour and marvelled that we had got in and out again in the dark. We hired a taxi and drove round the island. I didn't say anything about the leak. I pumped the bilge when no one was looking.

Flores was primitive and beautiful - the last island on the continent of Europe. The hedgerows along the narrow roads were ablaze of wild hydrangeas, the fields all pink and blue with flowers, breathtaking views of lush, forested valleys. The rock face along the shore was pitted with deep caves; the coastline carved by the sea into strange, monolithic sculpture. The people were poor; the farmers worked small, square plots of rented land, oxen dragging wooden ploughs, carts with solid wheels all fastened with wooden pegs. The fishermen set lobster traps round the precipitous shores and within the caverns and fissures that the sea had carved out. There was plenty to eat, much singing and music in the bars by the harbour at night, much railing against landlords and officials who batten on those who work. They still hunted whales in slender pulling boats - beautifully fashioned, lithe, almost fragile hulls powered by ten men pulling at long sweeps, with stout Samson posts fore and aft, all grooved by the harpoon lines; the harpoons themselves thrown by hand, the ironwork forged on the island, the ash staves delicately fashioned, finely balanced. Their only link with the mainland was a ship, the *Cavalheiro Arujo* which made the round trip from Lisbon to the islands of the Azores, including Madeira, every two weeks. She was a fine old steamer, carrying first class and second class passengers, livestock in the forward welldeck and cargo to and from the islands. She had been built in Glasgow some time before the war;

her steam reciprocating engines ran smoothly and silently. The islanders had few contacts with the world outside, many of them had never been to the mainland of Portugal. A strange vessel was an event worth switching on the leading lights for.

I could think of nothing but the leak. It seemed to be consistent - if it remained consistent and *Girl Stella* was pumped every watch it would not be dangerous. It justified anxiety, which I would have to bear, but not alarm. If we ran into a strong gale she would have to be nursed through it without allowing her to strain herself but there was no reason to believe that it was dangerous. I knew I ought to tell Celia about it but I said nothing, some deep-seated mechanism inside me holding back the words. I mentioned to Dick that she seemed to be making more water and would need pumping more frequently. He accepted this with his usual calm neutrality. It would be a major job when we got back to England. We returned to Porto Piqueran late in the evening, tired and brimming over with impressions of this lovely island. We had eaten ashore at the café by the harbour, had drunk bottles of Portuguese wine with the pilot and his friends, had discoursed far into the night. Earlier we had bought a few stores and fresh provisions in the village. 'We'll go tomorrow,' I said.

Porto Piqueran was still and quiet, only the constant swell and surge moving *Girl Stella* back and forth against the pull of her ropes. It was heavily overcast now; the stars together with the wind had gone. I checked the ropes again before we all went to bed - when they were asleep I pumped the bilge. I lay in my bunk, looking up at the deck-head, aware of a disquiet which kept sleep away. I had experienced this before, on this voyage and on others. It was the responsibility which I could never shake off or share. I felt aloof, shut up in an emotion-proof box, my fears shut up with me, my real feelings, even my hopes. I was a prisoner of my own restraint, taught by my upbringing never to betray fear or love or hate or to reach out for support from those who are close to me. There was an inevitability about this night which I was aware of, afraid of, but which I was unable to communicate. I slept fitfully for a few hours and then I heard the dinghy bump gently against *Girl Stella's* stern. I knew then that the play had begun to unfold. From that moment the itinerary of disaster gathered its own momentum.

The dinghy had been tied to *Girl Stella's* stern, streaming out with the westerly wind. If it was alongside, bumping against her

8

hull, it could only be because the wind had changed. I lay in bed digesting this information for a few moments, the chill news spreading its impulse through me. I got out of my bunk, put my head up through the companion way. There was a thin, wet drizzle, a light breeze slanting the raindrops from east to west. I put on my oilskin over my pyjamas, went on deck and moved the dinghy painter from the stern to the bow where it trailed out with the breeze under *Girl Stella's* bowsprit.

'When the rain comes before the wind,
Tops'l sheets and halyards mind'

I said to myself. I went below, tapped the barometer. It gave a convulsive jump downwards. I got dressed, called Dick. 'The wind's changed.' I said. 'We ought to get her turned round.' Dick got up reluctantly, looked out of the hatch. 'We can't do much in this,' he said, 'it's as black as a cow's inside. Wait till morning.' He went back to bed, was asleep in seconds. I made coffee, sat at the cabin table with the hot cup between my hands, the acrid steam swirling round my face. Dick was right. There was no chance that we could get through the entrance passage in this blackness. I was jumping to conclusions again, expecting the worst before it was due. We'd turn her at first light - that would be in good time and then, if it did freshen, we could slip and go. If it blew a gale we could scuttle round the island and lie in the lee until it was all over; we would ride out the gale in calm seas, no danger of too much leaking, then get on our way. Yet I knew Dick was wrong.

I tapped the glass again - it fell again. We ought to be on deck now. Turning her in the tiny space of Porto Piqueran would be difficult - a thousand times more difficult if there was wind. We ought to get her turned now while it was still calm, move the good ropes so that they held her bow the other way - pointing into the wind, pointing towards the sea. Why didn't I wake him, insist on doing what I knew was right? They'd all wake up, they'd all complain; they'd all think I was an idiot fussing about nothing. Why could I not do what I knew was right? Weak fool. I waited, searching for the morning, for the first streaks of the day. The wind increased with a steady purpose.

When it came, the dawn was a poor thing, a pale tint of light spreading over the unwilling sky, reluctant to displace the blackness of the night. I called Dick again. 'Come on, Dick. we must get her out of here - it's going to blow.' He got up at once and together we set about the business of turning *Girl Stella* round. The ropes ahead had to be let go from the rocks where the pilot had fastened them, then led round her bow and joined to one of the stern lines so that when we cast off the other she would cant round in her own length and face the entrance to the cove. There was no room to turn her in any other way. We worked together methodically.

Dick is the. best seaman I know. He knows what to do instinctively and wastes no time. He knows how to improvise, he is strong, agile, uses his brain. I started the engine; Celia and the boys got up. The wind was fresh now and the swell was rolling into Porto Piqueran; low cloud covered our world like a tight lid, below it the black squalls of a rising storm swept towards the west, swept into the cove. To seaward the waves were breaking over the rocks, already waking themselves to a sullen anger. *Girl Stella* was pitching and snatching at her ropes, the young waves crashing against her transom and sending spray over her stern. 'All right Dick - let go.' I shouted. He threw off the last rope forward and ran aft to join her bow line to the stern line. I saw the wave building up astern. It crashed against her, the stern line lifted out of the sea and came bar tight; it stretched taut, quivering, vibrating, the water squeezing out of it as the strain pulled it apart. I saw it before it happened. It broke with a dull thud, the bare end flying back.

I slammed her into reverse, gave her full throttle. The propeller raced, *Girl Stella* shook, black smoke poured from the exhaust. The engine held her. She began to move astern. I spun the wheel, she answered. 'Come on you poor bastard - come on, you'll do it.' She began to gather her way astern. I saw from the stone steps thatshe was moving backwards. We all watched her, mesmerised - the boys, Dick, Celia standing on the companion ladder, her face grey, anxious. Destiny was poised over us, the knife-edge of fate. In some way I knew that the course of my life would be fashioned in these brief seconds. If we could get to the corner we could slam her ahead and she would have room to come round, room to gather way so that she would answer the helm and steer clear through the entrance channel. I knew where the rocks lay. I had been round in the dinghy and plotted them, fixed their position in my mind. 'Come on you lovely old girl.' Then the bare end of the broken rope fouled *Girl Stella's* propeller. The engine stopped. It was over.

It was the end of her. I knew I couldn't save her, knew that she had moved out of my own or anyone's capacity to halt her destruction. We all went through the charade but we knew that nothing we could do would alter what was to be. We tried to cushion her against the rock face, we tried to cut the rope from her propeller, we ran another line to the steps to pull her free but she would have none of it. With the rising gale behind her she drove into Porto Piqueran. She hit the rocks with sickening, heart-breaking force. They drove their black teeth through her planking, ripped and tore her apart; the sea came into her and drew her down into its own mysterious world of darkness. For a few minutes her two masts protruded above the waves, two burgees fluttering a brave farewell and then they too disappeared. She had come as far as she would come and in Porto Piqueran she would rest.

We swam ashore to the stone steps, the boys and Celia in their lifejackets hand over hand along a rope, Dick obstinately trying to save our valuables until the last second of her life. When it was all over I remember standing on the quay - wet, cold, exhausted, counting heads. One - two - three - four. They were all there, all ashore, all alive. I felt a weight lift from me. It was over, all over. This conflict, within myself and outside as well, was resolved. We stayed on the island of Flores for a week waiting for the *Cavalheiro Arujo* to take us away.

A few days later she broke up and floated to the surface

11

II

Iskra

I don't know how he came to be there; perhaps his chubby, cheerful visage was fashioned by the shipwrights who built *Iskra* as a joke, or to please her first owner. Perhaps he came later, lovingly carved by an owner with a sense of humour. I can trace him back some twenty-five years; before that no records exist of the Dolphin, or, for that matter, of *Iskra* herself except her year of birth. A fire in Hillyard's yard in 1936 destroyed all written evidence of her building. Perhaps the Dolphin rose up out of the sea and fastened himself at her stemhead under the bowsprit, taking her as his home as a hermit crab takes to a shell. He has given her a part of himself. Without him her line is stark, formal, severe; he softens her, brings her a touch of fun, gives her a skittish lift which transforms her looks. I have always believed it is the quality of humour that carries *Iskra* through when times are rough. I can feel it in her. There is a suggestion of wisdom, too, in the Dolphin's wide-set eyes, his broad forehead, even the zany grin carries the hint of a deeper concern for our safety and welfare. He is like a Buddha, at once genial and grave. His fins, his curved body, his flat tail all suggest the swift movement that I have come to expect of *Iskra* - her ability to sail herself out of trouble, her instant response to a sudden demand, her dogged capacity to keep going, week on week, month on month. The Dolphin imparts to her the intelligence which is his birthright, which he inherits from his kind.

Iskra was the first boat I looked at after *Girl Stella*'s loss. I had asked the yacht broker for a gaff cutter made of wood, about 30 ft. long with a diesel engine. It had to be a boat I could sail alone. I named a modest sum which was what I could afford. 'We've nothing like that I'm afraid.' he said in the haughty manner of yacht brokers who sense a client with limited means, giving me a sheaf of lists and photographs and details of boats spread up and down the east coast of England. *Calva*, as she was then named, was tucked away unnoticed somewhere at the bottom. I bought her not because she fulfilled a dream but because she would serve my purpose. I didn't think much of her that first day I saw her. I believed that no boat I could ever own again would compare with *Girl Stella*. She had been so near to perfect that by comparison

12

anything else would be dross. It was later that *Iskra* unfolded to me her strengths, her virtues. She was one of dozens hauled out in the yard waiting for a buyer. She was covered over with an old tarpaulin - run down, unloved, dirty, hopeless. I first saw the Dolphin when I took the cover off. He looked incongruous, even ridiculous, up on her bow. The bowsprit, which gives him his roof, his frame, his own place in *Iskra's* outline, was off her and he poked himself up into the autumn sunshine like an appendage stuck on as an afterthought. 'I'll have that off her,' I said to myself - I don't want that junk.'

For a year I had been on the beach with no boat. I dug the garden, attended to my business, nursed my humiliation. There was no absolution. Whatever the mitigations, the special circumstances, the pleadings in my favour, I alone had to take the blame. If I had acted otherwise, with more caution, proper foresight, a keener judgement, it would not have happened. It is the ancient law of the sea and it is a just law. A thing of worth and beauty had been destroyed. Those last black hours of *Girl Stella's* existence, as error piled on miscalculation, chased themselves round the corridors of my mind, swelling instead of diminishing with the passage of time and becoming more vivid, more insupportable. It was as if all the errors of a lifetime had concentrated themselves into those brief hours. The wreck of the *Girl Stella* struck at the core of my ego, worried at the frayed edges of my mind. There was no way out; I would make the voyage to Cuba again, retracing my course mile by mile across the ocean in order to purge myself of a stain that would otherwise colour the rest of my life. This time I would do it alone. I no longer had the confidence to put others at risk under my command. The responsibility this time would be undivided. I believed I had no choice.

Attitudes change at once. The Master of a ship, however small she might be, has a position in life, an indefinable dignity bestowed on him by his charge. It is part of the fascination of the sea. A ship gives a man something, makes him bigger, stronger, wiser perhaps than he would otherwise be. Even a contemptible man, a worthless waster of a man, if he becomes the Master of a ship is given a standing that his character alone would never aspire to. A ship is a miraculous marriage of the material with the spiritual, a fashioning together of wood and iron and copper and rope and canvas to create a thing at once of joy and sorrow. A ship can be loved or hated, can respond to a man's touch with willing obedience, eager to give of her best, or she can be perverse, wayward, obstinate, sullen. A captain who loses his ship loses all that the ship gave him, finds himself stripped of distinction and reduced to the level of other men - reduced below them because he becomes the subject of contempt, pity, or thinly disguised ridicule. He loses his power when he loses the partner who gave that power, he becomes a master without a servant.

A ship is a microcosm of the world at large, with its own society, discipline, rules, conventions, its own routine. Each person has his possessions about him, the trappings of his life, all familiar and all contributing to his welfare and, indirectly, to the welfare of the ship. It has a settled order, an unvarying sequence of events which is in some way satisfying in itself. A shipwreck shatters this coherence. In minutes, perhaps, or hours, the fabric of life is destroyed, leaving nothing behind but the crew, with their lives if they are lucky. A ship I served in, during the last war, was torpedoed by a submarine in mid-Atlantic. In half an hour our lives were transformed, order was plunged into disorder, routine into chaos. There was nothing to show for what had been but a line of bubbles in the sea, an oil slick, a few smashed remnants of flotsam soon to be dispersed in the ocean. The unity which existed, where each person had his work, his contribution to make within the rigid framework of the ship, evaporated in seconds. Some helped their fellows, others looked only to themselves; some survived, others perished. The shock of it never left me.

The shock of losing *Girl Stella* did not wear off, it became worse with the passage of time. By a legal twist the insurance company managed to pay me no more than half *Girl Stella*'s value - just enough to buy *Iskra*. This voyage, like all my voyages from then on, would have to be on a shoestring. I have always been able to turn my boats to some financial advantage, otherwise I could never have owned and maintained them. *Iskra* would probably be willing to earn me an honest penny, either through her own efforts or through her ability to create saleable stories. As a beginning, her name would have to be changed. 'Calva', in Spanish, means 'bald', so that 'una calva' would be 'a bald woman' - not a suitable name for a boat sailing to Spanish-speaking Cuba. I hit on *Iskra* by chance. It is a Slav word meaning a spark or a small flame. It was the name of Lenin's first revolutionary newspaper, published in Vienna in 1912 - fitting enough, I thought, to sail to revolutionary Cuba and fitting my mood of that moment. It was the time of Vietnam, the Cuban blockade, the Bay of Pigs - a time to fly the standard of revolution if ever there was one.

Iskra was there, and at the right price, so I bought her. She didn't seem ideal for my purpose but I thought I could make do with her. She was too heavy for single-handed sailing, her gear was complicated and would be difficult to manage in heavy weather. She was too big to be easily handled by a man alone. Her engine was old enough to qualify for a museum, her cockpit drained into the bilge. I believe it was her underwater shape I fell for; the way the bulk of her is for'ard of amidships, tapering sweetly to a fine entry under her spoon bow; the way her lines sweep up towards her stern, giving her a concave section aft like the opening petals of a spring flower. It seemed to me that so fine a stern would leave no bad water behind. There is nothing fussy about her, no overhangs. She has a lift to her underwater lines that told me she would be kind to me when times were rough. She is all boat from stem to stern. As for the rest, I would somehow learn to live with her shortcomings.

With hindsight I understand that fortune did me no bad turn when she took *Girl Stella* away from me - I would have been broken by her in the end. She was too big, too expensive for me to have kept through these last lean years. A man who buys a boat that is too big and too expensive buys a treadmill. Like a beautiful woman, she will have him working his heart away to keep her in finery. From the moment she takes the water she costs money. There is hardly a corner left in all this sophisticated world where a boat can live free of dues - they become ruinous with a boat's size. Anyone can afford a couple of pounds a night, but at thirty pounds the joke turns sour. The bigger she is the more a man must earn simply for her to exist. Start the business of maintenance - paint, varnish, antifouling, rope, new sails, engine repairs and the cost spirals dizzily upwards. Insurance charges on a big boat are enough to make a brave man blanch, or to make him take the risk of leaving her uncovered. She will need a crew to sail her, extra hands to paint her and keep her smart, all eating, drinking, carousing at his expense. When she is hauled on the slip the charge would keep a modest family for a month. He will find that for the act to stay together he must work and worry until he is a neurotic jelly of a man, unable to reap the joy of his investment. *Iskra* is small enough for me to do the work on her myself, she can be laid against posts and her bottom scrubbed and painted by me alone; she can be sailed by me alone; she can be laid up in the winter in some snug mud berth for a modest sum.

For me, there is something essentially fulfilling about doing things on the cheap; it satisfies a mean streak in me to walk to the next bus stop and save the fare, to find something I can use that someone else has discarded, to adapt, to improvise rather than to buy; to pick up mussels and clams, make nettle soup, catch a fish for supper. It is something I learnt in my youth when I suffered poverty - it will stay with me for the rest of my life. It amounts to an essential efficiency with regard to the resources we are able to dispose of which is the essence of seamanship. *Iskra*, although I didn't know it at the time, was the right boat for me.

David Hillyard was new to designing yachts when he built *Iskra* in 1930; he had not yet broken with a tradition that demanded of a boat the ability to beat back to harbour in a storm without an engine. Soon after her building, his yachts became fat in their quarters to accommodate motors and smart living quarters. The centre cockpit and a separate cabin aft for the owner and his wife satisfied the desires of the new middle-class yachting fraternity on which his fortunes as a designer and builder depended. He was quick to develop the trend and his yachts soon increased in popularity. After *Iskra* they became good, comfortable, solid, safe, slow and boring, as they remain to this day.

Iskra wasn't boring when I first took her to sea. It was the end of the season, winter was already beginning to show its teeth. I wanted her back from the river Orwell, where I bought her, to Maldon, where I live. When she is at home in winter she lies with her bow to the quay outside the sailmaker's loft, gently lifting and dropping on the tide. It is a friendly, almost a rural place. My Dolphin looks out on a grassy slope, a pile of odd timber, an old lean-to shed, an upside-down boat and the massive timbers of the quay, the same now as they have been for two centuries. A wise old rat inhabits the nooks and burrows of the yard, passing the time of day and exchanging experiences with my Dolphin. I knew that once she was there I could work on her and try to make of her the boat I wanted for sailing across an ocean by myself. As soon as I got her outside the river Orwell and into the rough, brown waters of the Thames Estuary it came on to blow smartly from the south-west. This would tell me more about her than all

A wise old rat, the friend of my Dolphin

the previous owner's discourse or the yacht broker's flowery language, or my own observation of her hauled out in the yard.

She was heavy - heavy on the helm. As the wind strengthened she began to pull like a startled horse. Heavy to heave the mainsail, which was badly cut and sagged to leeward. Heavy to haul the jib sheets and to change the jib which set from the end of a twelve foot bowsprit. Heavy to reef alone, with roller reefing which needs two people. Heavy to swing the engine with a heavy iron flywheel and a flat battery. Heavy to hoist the anchor and chain with no winch. If I were to set off in this boat by myself, rigged as she was, I would be dead of heart failure within a month or become a superman.

There is a size of boat for every man, an equation between comfort and handiness that every lone sailor must solve for himself. His boat must be big enough for him to live on board in dignity, with space for a companion if he should meet one who fits. He should be able to stand, to move about freely, to have space for his belongings - clothes, books, pictures, trinkets, which all contribute to his completeness as a person. She must look like a home, feel like a home; she must give off the subtle aroma of peace that distinguishes a home from a perch. If, for good measure, she is built of wood, this is a bonus. Wood is a forgiving substance that breathes and lives and is born of the earth and the air and the warm sun. It is pleasant to live with. If she can be of heavy displacement this is another bonus. A heavy boat moves with grace and purpose, rocks a man's soul so that it is at one with the ocean. A light boat is a nervous creature, shying and flinching from the sea, jumping, shaking, restless and fevered. Equally, a boat for a single-hander must not be so big as to be a handful. He must be able to sail her into a crowded place without striking fear into those already berthed, be able to reduce sail in a gale and change a headsail without exhausting himself. Above all, he must be able to handle the anchor, the heaviest single piece of equipment on board. He must be able to lift it without help, stow it and get it ready. The size and weight of anchor he needs is also the limiting factor on the size of his boat.

Iskra showed me her virtues too on that first passage and I began to love her, though slowly at first. She was stiff, she was dry, she was safe, she sailed fast. She wasn't close winded because her sails were badly cut and badly designed. She dragged behind her a huge three-bladed propeller - she would be faster without it. She came through stays with an easy grace, never losing her way and never falling off when the wind caught her on the new tack. Her motion was steady; she never banged into a head sea, she would look after herself if I left the helm. As she began to tack across the Wallett, eating up the miles to windward, in a subtle way she insinuated herself into my favour. She showed me a quality of persistence which suggested to me that she would flog through anything that came her way until the end of time if I asked her to. She was clearly a better boat than I had taken her for. Given the chance, she seemed to be telling me, she would show me a thing or two. She was a better boat than anyone else had ever taken her for, I believed. She was a Black Beauty of a boat - a thoroughbred tied to the shafts of a hansom cab for too long. Give her a shorter boom, shift a few pigs of ballast and the heaviness would come out of her helm; give her a well-cut mains'l and she would point keenly instead of sagging dispiritedly to leeward; give her a chance and she would blossom. She might be the wrong side of forty but there was a prank or two left in her. When I eased the sheets in the Blackwater she flew up the river as if she was homeward bound.

I had fallen, too, for the friendly comfort of her. Her cabin was like the drawing room of a cottage in the country. Her old oil lamps were each held in place by two more dolphins to match the fellow on her bow. Her settee berths needed new covers but they had the deep comfort of age. She had a wide chart table, big enough to use for proper, ocean navigation, book shelves behind. The cabin was an airy place, lit by portholes and a well-proportioned skylight. At the same time I could see how snug it could be made when times were inclement outside. The galley would have to be rebuilt but it was spacious enough and it could be provided with a seat you could not be thrown out of. She had a little round mirror with a bevelled edge, framed in dark, old, rich mahogany. The cabin sides were of teak. The fo'c'sle had another wide, cosy bunk, and racks for sails, spare rope, shackles, blocks, spunyarn. Even then, before I had given her anything of my own, she looked like home.

As she lifted to the short, rough seas she creaked and complained softly, speaking the language of ships, smelling, feeling as the little world of a ship feels. All the magic of it came back to me. A month before I had made a nostalgic purchase - a sewing set, palm and needle, beeswax, twine, sail hook, all in a canvas roll, when I had no sail to stitch, no ropes' ends to whip with palm and needle. Now I got it out and put it up on the bo'sun's shelf of my new ship. I was a complete person again.

The Dolphin, too, had redeemed himself into my favour. His face was all grey at that time, as if he, too had been under-rated all his life. Yet there was a hidden urge towards better times written on that face. He was like an old actor who knows his real worth and only waits for the part which will bring the audience cheering out of their seats. He had taken a few bucketfuls of Thames Estuary in the face that day but he looked confident - as if he were inclined towards hopefulness. A bit of attention would do him good as well. His grin, his eyes, his quiff, his tail were all of a oneness, with grey paint obscuring his personality. He was a hermit, clothed in the grey cloth of penitence. Clearly something could be done to cheer him up.

When I looked at the Dolphin as he sat with his blunt nose peering over the sailmaker's quay I realised that all three of us, *Iskra*, or *Calva* as she still was, and himself and myself, all three of us were on the edge of better times. We were set for adventure, for the spaces of the ocean, for a great lift of the spirit that would transform our lives, raise us up from despondency to the heights of achievement. It was the Dolphin that made me aware of this opportunity - a purification that would come to the spirit through solitude, a new freedom. The dear, dear Dolphin.

III

Refurbishing

The opposition began to clamour at once. 'You'll never do it - you've no experience of single-handed sailing '- it's crazy, dangerous, eccentric. The boat's too large, too heavy, too old. Suppose you get ill, fall overboard, injure yourself? What about us, left at home, without news for weeks, not knowing whether you are alive or dead? It's horrible - no consideration for your family, your friends.' There was very little, 'Good luck - God speed,' or so it seemed. I had to summon my reserves of obstinacy. I had always harboured this dream - Joshua Slocum had left his impression on me. Now it was as if what had always been ordained for me had become an immediate necessity, and I knew I could not be shaken from my resolve. Once I had sailed *Iskra* from the river Orwell to Maldon the talking, for me, was over. Equally, I knew that the strictures of the opposition were valid and that they were delivered only out of concern. It was true I had never sailed alone except in a dinghy, and once in *Girl Stella* when I had taken her off the mooring in Bradwell and sailed her out towards the open sea and back one fine, sunny day. It had been as much as I could do to hoist the mainsail by myself and get her back to the mooring without damage. It had been a unique and unforgettable thrill that had lodged itself in my mind, waiting its chance to come out into the open. It was true also that *Iskra* was old and heavy. If I had been able to design a boat for myself she would have been different. But *Iskra* was cheap and the limits of choice were within my pocket.

I found that there was a mystique attached to sailing alone which was easy to understand but difficult to justify. Wanting to be alone is regarded as eccentric because it runs contrary to human behaviour. Most people are never alone for more than a few hours, even a few minutes, at a time. People go through their lives without ever spending a day alone. Criminals are forced to be alone as an extreme punishment. Therefore it is logical to believe that there must be something essentially amiss with a person who chooses to be alone at sea for days, weeks, even months. Doctor Johnson said, 'No man will be a sailor who has contrivance enough to get himself into jail. For being in a ship is being in a jail with the chance of being drowned.'

Sailing alone may be more dangerous than sailing with a crew, but I believe only marginally so. Falling overboard is the most obvious hazard and therefore the one that is most carefully guarded against. I soon learned to use a safety harness and I provided *Iskra* with safety lines which I could clip the harness to and at the same time move freely about the deck - like a yard dog shackled to a long wire. It is unusual for people sailing in a crewed yacht to wear a harness every time they stir out of the cabin, yet a man's chances of being picked up if he falls from a yacht in the ocean, in bad weather or at night, are slim. Perhaps the chance of falling overboard is less for a man alone because he conditions himself to take special care.

The risks of being run down, in theory, are greater for a man by himself because there is no one to keep a look-out when he is asleep. I didn't know it before I started, but in practice I found that my increased concentration and my increased awareness of what was around me, which is a product of being alone, helped defend me from this danger. Over and over again I have been protected by an inner sensation of disquiet which brings me to the deck in time to avert a danger. I believe that the risk of injury through a fall or a burn, or a bone fracture, or the danger of illness, are the most serious threats to anyone at sea in a small boat. Here the man alone is at a serious disadvantage. An injury may incapacitate him so that his boat is left to the mercy of wind and weather. He may be unable to dress a wound or set a bone on his own person, he may be made helpless by illness and his boat founder on the rocks.

Iskra is heavy and old - sixty years is a great age for a boat. I often wonder how her planks and her timbers and frames can stay tight after all these years. She seems so strong; I watch her when she is pounding to windward through a gale, hurled against the unforgiving waves, her decks awash, seas sweeping over her; marvel how her old bones hold together. She had already made a return crossing of the Atlantic when I bought her. I have added another eight crossings to the score, with two voyages from England to Norway, one round the north of Scotland and another round Iceland for good measure. One of her frames has been replaced, one side of her coach roof has been reinforced - otherwise she is as she was when she came out of the yard in 1930.

She was no more than a production boat, pitch-pine planking on oak frames, copper fastened, iron reinforced floors. She was built in the days when good materials were plentiful, when good craftsmen were easy to find and when tradition decreed that a boat should be a work of art, demanding the best from everyone concerned with her. When new she cost £450. I know of at least two others of her vintage from Hillyard's yard which have survived. Perhaps it is her weight, the sheer volume of material that went into her that keeps her together. The combination of weight and strength together with an easy flowing line keeps her from strain. I believe she was well looked after through her youth.

In 1930 single-handed sailing was almost unknown, gaff cutters were meant for several strong men to handle, not one weak man by himself. The fact that *Iskra*'s gear is heavy to handle has helped keep her hull from punishment since I have owned her. I soon discovered that a man alone in a heavy boat cannot afford to allow her to carry too much sail. Even if she will stand it, he cannot. As soon as the wind freshens I reef, otherwise *Iskra* becomes too much of a handful for me. If I neglect this principle, I discovered, the strength required to bring her under control is more than I have.

That first winter I owned her I re-designed her gear so that I would be able to sail her alone. I gave her a powerful Aries self-steering gear. I cut two feet off the end of her boom, bringing the mainsail further inboard, making the boom lighter and the sail easier to handle. I had a new mainsail made, loose footed, with a mitre seam and ordinary point reefing. This sail makes *Iskra* efficient to windward, keeps the gaff from falling away, a common ill with this rig, allows easy and quick reefing and has taken much of her weather helm from her. I changed all the halyards to synthetic rope, thinner and at the same time stronger than the old cordage and it runs through the blocks with less friction. This, with a lighter sail, took much of the work out of hoisting and lowering. I could not and would not wish to dispense with her long bowsprit which balances her and allows a huge spread of sail in light weather, but I arranged the jib with a simple furling gear so that it can be spirited away, by means of a tripping line from the cockpit.

For ocean sailing I wanted a boat that could be reefed, or the mainsail taken down, without rounding up - a wet, sometimes dangerous operation in a strong wind. I believed that this was possible with the gaff rig provided the gear was suitably arranged. To this end I fitted twin topping lifts from the hounds, each with a snap shackle on the end of the boom, so that the lee one could be taken clear of the sail. I fitted vangs from the end of the gaff, down through bulls-eyes, one on either side of the boom, leading for'ard to the inboard end of the boom where they pass through jam cleats. In this way the sail is free of any encumbrance on its lee side when it is being taken down in a strong wind. With the sheet pinned in, the weight of the gaff brings the sail down when the halyards are eased, the weather vang is pulled tight through the jam cleat to keep the gaff from the after shroud and the sail drops while the steering vane keeps her on course. The lee vang acts as a lazy-jack, keeping the sail from flogging to lee'ard. There are few Bermudian-rigged cruising yachts of any size that can be reefed or the sail taken down in a strong following wind without rounding up.

I love the gaff rig because it is simple, because it looks beautiful and because it is more efficient in a yacht which is to sail across oceans. With the gaff rig the sail offers a better shape to the wind - square at the top where the breeze is found, instead of a narrow finger of sail waving back and forth like a rolled umbrella. With my gaff rig I carry a topsail, increasing sail area where I want it, where the wind is. With gaff rig the working sails are small, no huge Genoa to smother a man alone in a breeze of wind. But gaff rig in light airs, with topsail and a big headsail set from the bowsprit end to the masthead, can give more sail than Bermudian for the same waterline length. Gaff rig has no truck with mast slides to jam, the sail cannot foul stays and shrouds at the top of the mast, the halyards are of rope which is easy to replace or repair or turn end for end. A gaffer's mast will stand even if the shrouds, or a runner, break. A gaffer's rigging is slack, not tensioned, so that it can be repaired or replaced by any good improvisor. There is something satisfying about the honest gaff, a certain complex simplicity, worn to its purpose through hundreds of years of evolution, sound, unpretentious, workmanlike.

Yacht designers went overboard for the Bermudian rig when new materials made tall masts and light displacement boats possible. With the tunnel vision common to specialists and experts they abandoned the gaff, concentrating their energies, successfully it must be said, on making yachts that would sail close to the wind. Fine old boats had their masts ripped out and replaced with Bermudian rig, making cumbersome, slow and unhandy vessels out of good sailers. No thought was given to the suitability of the rig for the hull. I once owned one of these boats - she was a travesty and an offence against the precepts of seamanship. The gaff was forgotten except by a few cranks and traditionalists who continued to sail their old boats and continued to find them to their liking. Until recently, when designers are being forced to understand its advantages, no effort or thought or application of technology was applied to the gaff rig. But sailing close to the wind, although it may speed racing yachts round the buoys, is not the be all and end all of yacht design. A yacht sailing the oceans spends a tiny proportion of its life hard on the wind. Like the old masters who developed the clipper ship, still a pinnacle of human achievement, the yacht sailing the oceans uses the world's wind currents to its advantage, still following the old routes which took square-rigged ships to every corner of the world without ever sailing closer than six points to the wind. In fact a modern gaff rig, contrived with no more than a measure of the expertise which has been showered on the Bermudian rig, will sail remarkably close to the wind. I have watched *Iskra* luff her way past Bermudian-rigged yachts a quarter her age.

I spent the whole of a winter and most of the following summer preparing *Iskra* for her voyage to Cuba. I rebuilt her galley, gave her a gas stove, a sink with fresh and salt-water pumps, a seat where I could sit and reach my pots and pans and the cooking paraphernalia with no fear of being hurled out by a heavy roll or a sudden lurch. I organised the food lockers so that I could stow what I wanted and find what I had stowed. I made extra space for food under the bunks, extra stowage for a thousand things I might need. I gave her new settee berths, a new cabin table, a workshop in the fo'c'sle with a vice, extra book shelves, a good shortwave radio, a position for my sextant which Dick had saved from the wreck of the *Girl Stella*. I fitted her with an extra inside compass, a grid steering compass which I can move from one position to another and clip to the bulkhead beside either bunk or in the centre of the cabin where I can see it at all times. I had twin staysails made for running in the trades, sun awnings for the tropics. She was still a heavy old boat when I had finished but there was no single task on board her which I was not strong enough to perform.

I spent the lonely months of preparation scheming out devices to make *Iskra* handleable by me alone. It took me the winter and most of the following summer to do all I had to do before I could set off - I suppose it was one of the most productive periods I have ever spent in my life. In that ten months I wrote the major part of my book about Cuba, *In Granma's Wake*, and deposited the manuscript with the publisher; I transformed *Iskra* from a run-down old gaff cutter to a vessel capable of taking me across the ocean and back and I organised my business so that it would keep my family for the nine months I would be away. For myself, I contracted with a magazine to publish fortnightly articles on the voyage, which, together with odd bits of journalism, paid my expenses and paid for much of *Iskra*'s refit.

Transformed to a vessel capable of taking me across the ocean

I was lonely because I was at odds with those who were close to me. I suffered from a breakdown in communication. Loneliness has nothing to do with solitude, it is concerned with people. I have never been lonely in the ocean as I was during those months between *Girl Stella*'s loss and the moment I set out in *Iskra*. As the land fell away behind me, so the loneliness fell away like a discarded skin. I had feelings of resentment because I believed they should be with me in my enterprise, in spirit if not in person. I felt a deep guilt because I was leaving them; I was afraid inside myself because part of me believed that I would never come back. In the dark watches of the night I conjured up visions of the storm, of *Iskra* battling with the ocean, and wondered how I would bring her and myself through it. I had been concerned with the sea for long enough to have no illusions about its omnipotence. I found it impossible to contemplate a picture of myself, alone, in the midst of this fury - the image would not focus in my mind. I knew there would be gales in the ocean. In *Girl Stella* we had passed through one, not as severe as I was likely to find. Then we had been drawn together by a collective danger, closer to one another, mentally huddled together in our own defence. I remember that each time a wave crashed on board our eyes would meet, the apprehension we all felt passing from one to the other and diminishing as it was shared equally between us. I wondered to what quarter I would turn for comfort without them.

I became secretive about my voyage, regarding it as a personal thing which I refused to share. I might fail or give up before I was properly started I reasoned, therefore the fewer people who knew of the venture the fewer would be the confessions of defeat. I didn't know whether I would be able to manage *Iskra* by myself - I never sailed alone until the day of my departure, apart from that first day when I brought her home, a device I planned for myself to make it more difficult for me to back out. Once she was good and ready, with all her stores on board, the charts bought, I would find it difficult to cry off. I manoeuvred myself, consciously, into this position.

In truth I have never liked talking about my plans before I embark on them because I have never been certain I will be able to carry them out. I regarded the voyage as a trial of strength I couldn't afford to lose, I was thinking in terms of victory and defeat, a dangerous concept when applied to the ocean. Now, I believe, I have a more mature approach to my travels in *Iskra*. I am prepared to change my mind, to back out and turn for home if I am frightened. My family were resentful of my secrecy, not without justification; they took it as a slight on their discretion and good faith. I didn't want their help, or anyone's help. After I lost *Girl Stella*, self-sufficiency became my overriding ideal. Now I understand that I was lonely then because I refused to accept help, understand that it is easier to give help than it is to receive it graciously. The ocean has given me some understanding, more compassion, but it came too late. My relationship with Celia received a mortal wound when *Girl Stella* sank beneath the waves.

I was confident that I was well placed to make a second voyage to Cuba after the success of the *Girl Stella*'s visit. Her voyage had been something of a triumph, apart from its disastrous ending in Flores. We had spent three months in the island and made friends among officials, even ministers. This time I intended to sail along the north coast to Havana; I would make my first landfall at the little port of Baracoa in the extreme east. At that time the revolution was only ten years old and the coasts of Cuba were dangerous. There were frequent terrorist or, more respectably, guerilla raids on the island, usually mounted from the Bahamas, close to the north. The Cuban defences were on the alert and were said to be more inclined to open fire on any strange small craft found within their territorial waters than to stop and ask polite questions. I wanted to be sure that they would know about *Iskra*'s arrival - I gave them a date and a time. This was not as difficult as it might appear. With the trade wind consistent and in my favour I could arrange things so that I arrived in the neighbouring island of Hispaniola a few days before I was due in Cuba. From there I could easily make my departure so as to arrive in Cuba on time.

Fidel Castro's revolution was still fresh and unsullied by the power game. It was clearly a true movement of the people, an expression of hope and faith. The story of the revolution is romantic, fascinating, especially so to me, with my experience in Latin America where I lived as a child and being of a romantic disposition. It captured the imagination. The charismatic young Fidel Castro fighting for freedom and principle against the corrupt, unsavoury dictatorship of Fulgenio Batista and winning against all the odds is a modern fairy tale. The landings near Santiago, in the shadow of the Sierra Maestra which we had seen as *Girl Stella* came up with the southern shores of Cuba, the battle where all but a biblical twelve of the one hundred strong invasion force of exiled patriots were killed or captured, the slow, painstaking build-up of strength and confidence among the peasants of the Sierra; all these were powerful ingredients in a story of compelling excitement.

I had followed the Cuban Revolution from its inception, had been outraged with thousands of others by the Bay of Pigs invasion and had trembled with millions at the missile crisis. When I found myself with an ocean-going vessel at my disposal and the means to make a voyage I seized the chance to go and look at Cuba, try to find some truth from among the conflicting tales that came out of the island. To some, Fidel Castro's revolution was the millenium; to others it was a worse oppression than had preceded it. The reality must lie somewhere in between. I did not know when I went that I would be forced to make the voyage over again. I did not know that it would lead me into the labyrinth of solitude, that it would change my outlook, my attitude to the world around me, my appraisal of myself; that it would destroy one relationship and form another, would change my way of thinking and living, would change my understanding. Just as the ocean wears away the rocks and bends the contour of the shore to its will, so it washes over a man's mind, smoothing the sharp edges, knocking off the conceits, flattening the prejudices so that he is left with a different instrument with which to govern his life.

IV

Strange Happenings

My Dolphin had a new coat of paint - now his fins, his tail, his eyes, his wide mouth with the zany grin, were set off in black against his grey body. He looked smart, self-assured like a businessman on his way to the office, all shaved and shiny, set up to face another day's journey through the commercial jungle. For a week he had listened to the whine of the west wind as it howled round the top of the mast, tearing at the gaunt trees that sustain themselves precariously round the top of the Guernsey yacht marina. Sometimes a rogue eddy would come sweeping down among the moored yachts, tugging at ropes, worrying at canvas covers, grinding together the iron pontoons. My Dolphin shuddered inwardly. Soon he would be taken away from this cosy berth, forced to face the ocean outside those protective walls of rock, ejected into the cold sea and the biting wind. It would be better to stay where he was. He had no stomach for punishment.

After a week the wind eased, veered to the north. Now there was no reason not to go. The stores were bought and stowed in the lockers, the tanks full, the family gone home, leaving me to ponder the extent of this folly while the gales penned *Iskra* inside Guernsey marina. It had been no grand, haughty, sweep of a decision - 'I'll sail alone across the ocean.' Rather a seed, a fertile, assertive weed, had taken root in my mind and swelled until it filled all the spaces with this one resolve. One small whim, laid on another, had grown into this obsession. I had kept it to myself for a long time, hoping perhaps that it would go away but soon it was out, known to my friends. Dick had left a bottle in *Iskra*'s cockpit the night before she sailed from Bradwell, with a note: 'Good luck, Frank'. There could be no turning back.

It was a cold, bright day in September 1970 when *Iskra* left the Guernsey marina. White clouds like huge pieces of jigsaw were striding across the sky from north to south. The sea was rough after the gale. *Iskra* marched through it, throwing it carelessly away from her bow, stinging spray flying across the deck. Bert Le Nury had let go my ropes. 'Where are you bound?' 'Cuba.' 'What?' he said, 'good God.' He took my hand in his great maw and shook it. 'Good luck.' Then I was alone, the rocks of the Platts Fougière behind me, the island of Guernsey already a dream, the whole of life a dream except this moment which was reality. Yet I felt a kind of unreality, as if I were someone else, separated from this person standing in *Iskra*'s cockpit. I looked all round the boat, in the fo'c'sle, the cabin, the lavatory, even under the chart table to see if this other person was there - but he wasn't. I shouted out 'Hey, Frank' quite loud, but the sound went on its way, bringing no answer, no echo, dissolving itself into the wind and sea.

Iskra steered herself under her vane, the ropes and chains pulling and easing by a clever magic of their own. When I turned on the gas to light the kettle I saw my hand shaking. I knew what to do. I had prepared everything before I left the marina, laid off the course on the chart, unshackled the anchor, sealed the hawse in the deck, put away ropes and fenders. I turned on the radio and a voice came out. It seemed to be speaking a strange language I didn't understand, discussing matters that had no relevance to me. I turned it off, went out into the fresh breeze and looked round the horizon. Ahead there was nothing but ocean, merging into sky far away. Behind, the island of Guernsey was diminishing in size. I put a tape on the cassette player, turned it up loud. The sound poured out - beautiful sound, special sound to meet a special moment, a fantasy of invention to match a fantasy of experience, a miracle of order to bring order into a scattered mind. This was reality, this was my world - Mozart, Schubert, fitting together the misplaced pieces. As I listened to the music I began to occupy myself and the two separate people began to merge back into one person.

I took a sun sight at noon and crossed it with a bearing of the island which I could still faintly see astern. I cooked myself lunch. I looked at the paper I had bought before leaving the marina. I worked an estimated time for *Iskra* to arrive at Ushant when I would turn her south across the Bay of Biscay. I opened a new exercise book and began to write my journal, which I kept every day and which I still keep every day when I am on my own at sea. The journal helps to keep these two people together. *Iskra* was going at her top speed with all plain sail in a fresh breeze. Sometimes she would slap against the steep seas and a curtain of spray would sting across the deck. More often she avoided them, cleverly twisting and turning herself so as to slide easily through them. It was good to watch her. I would be in Spain within five days; perhaps I would miss out La Coruña and sail direct to Vigo;

perhaps I would call in at some of the lovely Rias of Galicia I knew so well from past voyages. We had been to all of them in *Girl Stella* and I had many friends there. It wasn't so bad to be alive, perhaps. I was on my own with *Iskra* and my Dolphin, my shoreside responsibilities fast melting into the haze astern. They had been tormenting me for years. Now they could look after themselves for a spell. Now I could please myself.

In the evening the barometer began to drop. The sunset was hard, yellow, putrid, the wind backed a point. I changed *Iskra* to a small jib, put two reefs in the main as the wind freshened. Soon she was close-hauled as the wind headed. Soon she could not steer the course. She began to labour to windward. When it got dark the seas increased in size; now they had white caps. She began to strain. I put in a third reef. Now the deck was a lonely place, swept by heavy spray, sometimes a wave breaking aboard. I felt its force lift me as I worked up on deck by the mast, slacking the halyard, pulling down the luff of the sail, heaving on the reefing tackle, tying in the points. It was heavy work but all the gear is simple. Boats have been rigged in the way *Iskra* is rigged for hundreds of years; there's little to go wrong. From the mast I could see her as a dark outline, heaving herself up over the waves, forcing herself into them, straining to keep her forward movement, the empty cockpit, the sea streaming past the lee coaming, all flecked with white, the black sails etched against a dark, moonless sky.

I struggled with my loneliness. It would be good to have someone to shout to, to see a reassuring body watching me from the cockpit, even to know that someone was below, asleep perhaps, or making a cup of tea. 'I'm only here because I want to be here.' I said to myself over and over again, making a tune out of it: 'I'm only here 'cos I want to be here, I'm only here 'cos I want to be here ....' She was beginning to leak, a tell-tale line of bilge water already encroaching along the lee side of the cabin sole, drips of sea forcing themselves through the closed hatch, through the skylight, through the brass rims of the portholes. I cleared the bilge, working the pump in the cockpit until I heard it suck air. The lights of the French coast winked to leeward. She was getting closer.

As she was driven closer to the shore the strength of the tide increased, steepening the waves so that *Iskra* took them full in her face, shaking at the impact as she drove into them. At midnight I put her about on the off-shore tack. It was the first time I had

asked her to go through stays against a strong wind in a rough sea, the first time we had been in these conditions together. I wondered how my Dolphin was finding life, down there under the bowsprit. I disconnected the vane steering from the tiller and sailed her off the wind for a few moments allowing her to gather her way, then, judging a calmer patch, I slammed the tiller to leeward and held it hard over. She came shaking and slatting into the wind, held herself for an instant in its eye, pitching and dipping her bowsprit and then she came sweetly round on the new tack. 'You lovely girl,' I muttered as I handed the sheets.

I made myself a cup of soup and sat in the cabin with the mug warming my hands, the aromatic steam gently swirling upwards. I sat on the weather bunk, my feet braced across the cabin against *Iskra*'s shakes and shudders. The night was interminable. I was tired but I couldn't sleep through this discomfort, this cold, wet, long night. I listened to the sea outside, muffled like the noise of traffic in a city street; watched the inside compass on the bulkhead in front of me as it moved in its gimbal with *Iskra*'s motion. The two men were beginning to move apart again. 'What are you doing here?' one asked. 'It's what I want to do.' 'You're crazy, daft, softheaded, an idiot. Who would want to do this? There's nothing in it whatsoever that has a single vestige of commonsense. You could be at home - warm, dry, safe.' 'I want to do it.' The dawn came, spreading an unwilling, comfortless light across the wilderness that was the sea.

It blew all day and all the following night. I became like an animal, moving to do what I had to do mechanically out of instinct rather than volition. I pumped the bilge, I watched the compass, I attended to the navigation in a desultory manner, I made cups of strong tea, I ate biscuits, sweets, an apple, anything to hand. Sometimes I dozed uneasily, propped across the cabin with my feet hard against the opposite bunk. *Iskra* sailed on to windward with a dogged persistence. She crossed the shipping to the north and I saw the masts and outlines and lights of ships moving majestically on their way with studied indifference. I put her about again and she moved back across the line of ships until she came again close to the French coast, it seemed an imperceptible distance closer to Ushant. I sailed her offshore again in the night.

The other man was a real man now; I could almost see him in the cabin, a replica of me but wearing an old trilby and a brown macintosh, like an out of work private detective, huddled in a corner of the lee bunk. I could hear his voice now, resonant and clear, echoing round the recesses of my mind. 'Pack up and sail back to England on this tack - you'll fetch Falmouth with luck; don't go on with this madness - be a sensible chap, admit it when you've had enough.' I listened to him; perhaps I should go to Falmouth and take stock, pull myself together and then try again. It would be no more than commonsense. Then the wind moderated and veered to the north west. *Iskra* sailed past Ushant well to the west, I picked up its bleep on the radio direction finder and the wind died leaving her becalmed. I took the sails down and went to sleep.

I didn't understand what was happening to me at the time, but now I know that I was learning my lessons during that first hard blow with *Iskra*. When I woke up from my sleep I was a different man, at least as far as seamanship was concerned. The weather did me a good turn. It wasn't a real gale - I doubt whether the wind ever reached more than force 7 on the Beaufort scale, but it was hard enough to hammer home the lessons. I learned that if I was to sail alone I would have to organise my life so as to be able to withstand a spell of hard weather. I learned that, to windward, *Iskra* is far stronger than I am; that any well-found boat is stronger than any man by himself when sailing against the wind. I had been half stupid with fatigue for three days and two nights, an unnecessary and dangerous state. If anything difficult, anything requiring real judgement or more than average strength had been required of me I would have been incapable of it.

From that moment I evolved a method of sleep that should and usually does, keep me fresh and in charge of my faculties in all but the worst conditions. When I am sailing alone I sleep for an hour at a time, spreading my sleep periods over the twenty-four hours. I start this sleep routine before I leave harbour so that I am already used to it when the voyage begins. At first I found it difficult but now I fall asleep like a child and wake like a dog, at once alert and attentive. I eat regular, proper meals. If it is too rough to cook I have a vacuum flask of hot food, a ready-to-use bag of mixed nuts and raisins and some chocolate.

When I woke up from my sleep I was taught another lesson immediately after the first. A breeze came up from the north east and I hurried to make sail. *Iskra* was rolling heavily, the sails were lying untidily over the deck as I had left them before I went to sleep. I broke out the jib and she began to move briskly through the water. As I went for'ard to fasten the halyard to the head of the staysail I slipped on a loose fold of sail, the hauling part of the halyard flew out of my hand and sprang upwards where it twisted itself round and round a shroud high above the deck and out of my reach. By standing up on the furled mainsail with one foot on the sidelight screen and stretching out to the shroud I could just reach the end of the rope so that I could unwind it. Then *Iskra* gave a roll, my foot slipped and I fell. My leg grazed against the lifeline, she rolled again and I was in the water, spluttering and coughing.

Now she was moving at no more than strolling pace but it seemed faster. I grabbed for the rail as she rolled towards me. It was as if I was being dragged through the water at great speed. When she rolled back my fingers were torn free. I swam beside her as she sailed past. She looked huge, towering up out of the sea, her mast infinitely high, sweeping great arcs across the blue sky, her painted sides smooth, featureless walls, slippery with water, offering no hold. When I came to the stern I grabbed the rudder, reached up for the steering vane supports and clambered aboard. I went below and put on my safety harness. Now I never leave the cockpit without it.

Sailing alone is a continuous process which demands concentration day and night for weeks on end. A man alone becomes tuned to a high level of awareness. It is always dangerous at sea in a small boat, even when the wind is fair and the weather smiles there may be dangers at hand - a ship on collision course, a log or a piece of heavy dunnage in the sea which could damage the frail hull of a yacht, a black cloud on the horizon with a sudden squall in it. It is concentration that keeps the lone sailor alive. It gives him a heightened concern for his safety and the well-being of his ship; it is his early warning device, it raises his consciousness so that he lives on a plane where instinct and quick perception govern his impulses. Concentration makes him sensitive, strung up, with his mind on edge, able to see things before they happen. The fewer the mechanical aids he has the keener will be these perceptions; the more he is forced to rely on his own skill, judgement, intuition, the greater will be his ability to survive alone.

Iskra has no gadgets - in part because I am too mean to spend good money on them, in part because I know that anything depending on a supply of electricity is suspect in a small boat. Electricity and salt water are poor mixers. In *Iskra*, when the sea is rough and the wind hard, the element of salt water is so much a part of her, inside and out, that anything electrical has a poor chance of survival. She has electric lighting which I use occasionally, an electric pump and an electric depth sounder. I spend many hours of my life cleaning corroded contacts, tracing faulty wiring and replacing corroded fittings. I begrudge this time and know that it would increase in direct proportion to the gadgets shipped on board. On my last voyage over the Atlantic I had no batteries for a long spell and no means of charging them. I lived quite happily without the benefit of electricity and suffered no noticeable hardship.

The ocean is full of strange happenings. It stores up knowledge and surprises and releases them small piece by small piece when we are least expecting them, giving us strange, sometimes uncanny insights into ourselves. *Iskra* left Vigo in Spain early in October, bound for La Palma, the most westerly of the Canary Islands; I had been there before in *Girl Stella*. La Palma is a high, green island with spectacular scenery, its slopes criss-crossed with cultivation, the white and red houses stuck to the mountainside in a mosaic of colour. Off the Portuguese coast *Iskra* picked up the strong north wind known as the Portuguese trade wind and sped south with twin headsails set. It was the first time I had used these sails - they were an incomparable thrill.

I gained in confidence as she sailed south, falling into my new routine of sleeping in short snatches. At first I would set the alarm to wake me but soon I learned to wake myself. My body and my mind settled for an hour and a quarter. I would wake, check the time, glance at the compass by my bunk, listen, sense *Iskra*'s movement, gauging her roll and surge. Usually, but not always, I would get up and look round the horizon and round the deck before going back to sleep for another hour and a quarter. This is my life at sea now; I do it two or three times in the night and two or three times during the day.

Iskra made good time from Vigo - an average of 130 miles a day. I had seen nothing since leaving the Spanish coast. I had stopped using navigation lights in order to save oil, I had stopped hoisting my radar reflector because of the nuisance of it and because it would sometimes chafe the sails. I hadn't learned caution although I must have learned something about concentration. Six days out *Iskra* was near Madeira, in a line between that island and Lisbon.

I woke that night unexpectedly. I looked at the clock and saw that I had been asleep for only forty minutes. I looked at the compass - she was on course. I listened - nothing was to be heard except the swish of the bow wave, the creaks of the gear, the familiar knocks and shudders and rattles. I turned over to go back to sleep but found my mind was alert, racing, images of alarm flickering through it like a celluloid film strip. I got up, unable to be at peace, cursing myself for an idiot.

As soon as I got to the hatch I saw it - a bright red light coursing steadily and fast across the sky like a rocket or a satellite. Then I saw the iron slab of a ship's side hurtling past, heard the low hum of a steam engine, the sound taken away from me by the wind. I leapt for the tiller, slammed it over and *Iskra* spun away from the danger. As the ship rolled I could see the open portholes, the line of her boat deck, the wing of the bridge, then her rounded stern. *Cavalheiro Arujo - Lisboa*. I put *Iskra* back on course, lit the Tilley pressure lamp, hung it on the boom gallows where it shone a bright light all around the horizon and went back to sleep.

When I thought about this incident the next day, I was more struck by the strangeness of the coincidence that the *Girl Stella* should obtrude herself into my life again than I was frightened by the nearness of my escape. That I should almost be run down by the very ship that brought us all away from Flores after our shipwreck was astounding. I was so astonished by the coincidence of it that I failed to recognise the equally strange coincidence of two such infinitely small objects as a ship and a yacht, in the context of the ocean, being drawn together on a collision course. The significance of my waking up in time to avoid disaster did not at that time occur to me. I remarked in my journal for that day that I had not been frightened by the incident. I know that if I had come within inches of being run down by a car, or had escaped miraculously from a train accident or a fire, I would have shown signs of fear and shock.

It was when the next incident occurred, several years later, that I connected the two together. I was sailing alone from the east coast of England to Kristiansand in Norway. The North Sea is a busy place, not only with ships on their regular trade routes but with fishing boats from ports in England, Holland, Denmark and sometimes further afield, racing between their home ports and the fishing grounds round the English coasts. Fishing boats are notoriously bad at keeping a look-out. They set their self steering and belt through the night in the expectation that everyone else will keep out of their way - as I do myself. The difference between us is that I am weaker and more vulnerable than they.

I was asleep in the early morning, just after the dawn, having stayed awake through the short summer night. Visibility was about five miles. I had carefully scanned the horizon before going below for my regulation one and a quarter hours. I woke again, with the same sensation of unease; a tingling through my body, an alertness, the strange, insubstantial, but persistently nagging feeling that all is not well. I saw it as soon as I got to the hatch - a fishing trawler, probably Danish I thought, although she had no ensign flying, steaming at eight knots across *Iskra*'s bow. I held *Iskra* on course to see what would have happened. She would have poked her bowsprit through the wheelhouse window. I luffed her into the wind and the fishing boat thundered by within feet. There was no one in the wheelhouse; I could see through the deckhouse scuttle the men sitting round a mess table eating their breakfast.

These are not isolated incidents. I was on passage alone across the Atlantic from Sydney, Cape Breton, to Falmouth in 1982. I had seen only one ship on the whole twenty-three day voyage. She was called the *Encontrans Speed*, and she came up on one of the very few sunny days of the passage when I was sitting in *Iskra*'s hatch enjoying the welcome and unaccustomed warmth. I didn't see her. The first I knew of her was a voice coming through my VHF radio which is now always switched on. 'Hullo, yacht, what are you doing out here?' She was still astern of me, about half a mile on the quarter. There was no danger and therefore, perhaps, no feeling of apprehension. I spoke to the Chief Officer and he promised to send a message home for me, which gave a great lift to my spirits.

Ten days later I was in the approaches to the English Channel. It was shortly after dawn, I had been asleep for half an hour, *Iskra*'s navigation lights were burning bright. I woke up with 'the feeling', which is now familiar to me, and which I never fail to respond to. Occasionally 'the feeling', as I call it, is unjustified; I go up, look round and all is clear and well. Usually I find something amiss - a slack rope on the deck, a sail chafing, a loose shackle, an ugly cloud on the horizon, a change of wind putting *Iskra* off course. On this morning I could see nothing, but it was thick with a light, driven rain that cut visibility to less than half a mile. I made a cup of tea but the feeling persisted; I kept looking nervously out of the hatch. Then I saw it. At first I couldn't make it out. It was a huge double tower with a flat top and a tall crane waving through the mist. It looked like an oil rig - there are no oil rigs in the middle of the English Channel. Then I saw that it was an oil rig, under tow of a tug which loomed out of the mist. With luck *Iskra* would have passed between the tug and the rig.

It was a long time before I connected these isolated happenings to the theory, or perhaps the idea, which is well known and well documented, that a high level of concentration can give rise to extra-sensory perception. As if to emphasize the veracity of these incidents I went through another - a kind of control experience which gave to the whole affair the flavour of a laboratory experiment. *Iskra* was on passage between the island of Horta in the Azores and Falmouth, with Anne Little as crew. Anne is an experienced sailor in her own right and has made other voyages on board *Iskra*. When we were approaching soundings off the west coast of France we decided that as there were two of us, a luxury I had become unused to, we should keep a continuous lookout.

On this night I was sound asleep; Anne was on watch, sitting in the hatch as *Iskra* steered herself, a strong wind on the quarter, bright moonlight. She saw a fishing boat approaching, crossing ahead or possibly on collision course. Not wishing to wake me unnecessarily she watched while the fishing boat came closer and then woke me up. 'There's a trawler pretty close. You ought to have a look.' She found it difficult to rouse me. Not being alone I had been asleep for a full two hours, revelling in the luxury of having a crew on board. By the time I had dragged myself up to the hatch, rubbing the sleep out of my eyes, the fisherman was almost on us. *Iskra* had to be put about in quick time to avoid a collision.

Technology has failed to stop or even to reduce accidents at sea, where ships still collide with each other and with the rocks. The technical armoury of a modern ship is formidable sophisticated radar not only shows clearly on a screen when danger is approaching, but makes a loud, clamorous sound to warn of an imminent collision. There are devices to suit every contingency, yet accidents continue unabated. As two matchsticks floating in a bath will be drawn towards each other, so ships or yachts are inexorably pulled together in defiance of the mechanical odds against it. The most minute alteration of course or of the time scale would ensure that two vessels destined to cross in the ocean would pass miles clear. Over and over again they do not. There is some factor at work here that is not understood, some communication that is on a different plane from that of our technology.

When an expert golfer, encapsulated in his cocoon of concentration, sinks a putt at twenty yards he is using a power more potent that any mechanical aid, the simple ability to hold his club at the correct angle, which must be so precise as to be unmeasurable. When a cellist feels not only for the note but for an inflexion of the note, his own personal interpretation of it, he is using the same power, the same instrument of concentration that keeps a lone sailor safe at sea. It is the direct link between the mind and the end product, wrought by concentration to a pitch of perfection, undiluted by the intervention of mechanical aids. Dials, needle, flashing lights and clever gadgets are fallible. A man's unfettered senses, when his life depends on them, are a better warranty for his safety.

The mechanism that guides a flock of birds, allowing them to wheel and dive and climb in perfect unison; the mechanism that warns animals of danger before they are able to see or hear it, is at work inside ourselves if we will allow ourselves to use it. When I stand on *Iskra*'s foredeck as she sails through the trades and watch the dolphins round her bow I feel an affinity with these creatures. As a species, dolphins are said to be more intelligent than human beings. Certainly they are creatures of exquisite grace, perfectly fitted to their element. I feel a yearning to share in their magical, disciplined movement. They don't destroy the world they live in, they don't slaughter one another, they don't pollute the ocean, they don't squander their own environment, they don't collide with one another. As I look at my own Dolphin, tucked under *Iskra*'s bow, I understand that he is a distant, wooden cousin of my friends in the ocean; perhaps inheriting in his genes their unique intelligence, communicating to me something of their understanding. I am proud that he belongs to me and I to him.

V

Trial by Calm

I was thirty days in the ocean from La Palma to Antigua on my first single-handed voyage - my return to Cuba. It was a form of purgatory wherein I shed a part of my identity and took on another. What I took on is easier to live with than what I lost and therefore I have no regrets. I lost a little arrogance perhaps, gained a little humility, learned how to resist frustration. We do not change readily unless something of consequence happens to us; my first lone voyage across an ocean was of consequence to me. The human mind is a conservative instrument. It will persevere with its prejudices long after they have outrun their credible life, continuing remorselessly to hold opinions that have been overtaken by events. Facts change, people stay the same. The facts of living in our world change around us with alarming speed but we continue in the same mould, defying them with magnificent disregard. A single-handed voyage across an ocean should be mandatory for all who aspire to positions of power over others. It concentrates the mind remarkably. It teaches a man respect and love for the world he lives in, teaches him to know his own limits, makes him aware of the natural balance between himself and other living creatures which must be kept if man is to survive.

It was an auspicious day when *Iskra* left La Palma. The sun was shining, the barometer high, the wind fresh and steady from the north-east; I was rested and ready to go, *Iskra* was full of the best stores I have ever had on board. They came from an old man in La Palma who lives high up the mountainside where he cultivates a patch of land. I met him casually in a bar and struck up a friendship with him. He was fascinated by *Iskra*'s voyage. Don Felipe supplied *Iskra* with her fresh stores, straight from his own *hacienda* or from his friends' round about: vegetables with the garden soil still clinging to them, tomatoes graded from ripe to hard green, a hand of bananas, oranges, pineapples, melons from this most fertile soil, eggs fresh from Don Felipe's hens. When I arrived in Antigua thirty days later my vegetables were still better than any I could buy ashore. They were stored in slatted boxes on the fo'c'sle bench, where the light is shaded and where cool air circulates freely round them. *Iskra* has no refrigerator and has never needed one.

Don Felipe and his wife Dolores took me into their hearts. Dolore's sister Lourdes had gone to Cuba, twenty years previously, when she was a small girl. Dolores gave me her address in Havana and entrusted me with a gold locket on a chain which her mother had left for Lourdes. Because of the revolution Dolores had been frightened to send it in the post and I was to be its courier. They showered me with kindness. Don Felipe gave me two bottles of Spanish brandy. They wouldn't allow me to pay for the stores they provided and they came to the quay and watched *Iskra* leave, Dolores weeping as if she would break, as if I were her son leaving her forever.

It was the first time I had seen anyone weep for me. In some way it helped me to support the fear that took hold of me when I hauled in the anchor. I have always had this fear at the beginning of a voyage - it has never left me. At first I was surprised at it, now I know it always comes and have learned to expect it. Even so, the fear never diminishes. The moment I grasp the chain there is a clear, incisive break in the routine of life, the past disintegrating, the future full of uncertainty. The cards of life are placed face up on the table. I know now that the fear begins to leave me as soon as I am under way, slowly growing fainter as I become absorbed in the voyage.

Soon *Iskra* was under twin staysails, the coast of La Palma sliding past to starboard, the island of Hierro ahead, Gomera far away to port. She sailed 1,500 miles in her first ten days under twin staysails - the best and most exciting run I have ever made in her. The trade wind freshened to force 7 on the Beaufort scale and stayed true in direction and strength day and night. In accordance with its custom it would increase towards evening so that the twins had to be reefed and then ease again in the night. The boat was taut and drawn out like a bowstring, humming with strain. I worried for the gear, but it held. Halyards and stays, were bar tight, the sails rounded with wind as if they would burst. I feared for the top of the mast which was bending forward above the hounds where it is supported by the two wire backstays. I devised extra support for it with the peak halyard, taking the blocks off the gaff, fastening them to the rail and bowsing down on the hauling part to force the mast back.

It was like square rig; everything pulling with even, steady strain, the boat rolling with a regular, rhythmic swing, the tiller amidships, the course never varying more than two degrees either way, the log spinning off the knots - 140, sometimes 160 miles from noon to noon. The sun shone, the trade wind clouds built their castles of fantasy round the horizon's rim, the storm petrels skimmed the wave tops endlessly, back and forth across *Iskra's* wake; flying fish rose from the sea in green and purple clouds, flashing in the sun as they raced over the wave tops, the dolphins wove patterns in the sea ahead, leaping into the sunlight or blazing their paths in purple phosphorescence through the night.

I was caught up in the intoxication of this onward surge. I would sit for hours under the mast watching the sea hurtle past; watching the sails, the magic balance of strain and give and twist and roll, the graceful, onward dance that is a sailing ship in a strong following wind. The daily noon positions marched across the chart of the Atlantic Ocean with bold, purposeful strides.

I began to calculate *Iskra's* arrival in Antigua. In a week she was nearly half way across - at worst she would clip a couple of days off *Girl Stella's* time for the same voyage. It was a vindication of what I had worked for, an exultation. Here was everything I had devised working in perfect accord; every rope, wire, shackle that I had thought about and placed cunningly in position doing

My Dolphin's kith and kin leapt and cavorted all round him

44

precisely what I had ordained for it all the thought I had put into the project bearing fruit in this helter-skelter of progress. I could look around me and see that the whole affair of boat and gear and stores, all the convenience and comfort and sanity that surrounded me, were of my own making. It was something complete that I had started from the beginning and had brought to fruition through my own efforts, something I had done and was doing myself. All the emotional trauma of conflicting personalities that I had passed through, all the misgivings, the doubts, the fears, all the dire warnings, the arguments, the pleadings had been overcome. I possessed the skill and knowledge to do this and the determination to push through with it against all opposition. Here, in *Iskra*'s headlong rush towards the west, was the visible and tangible proof that it was all justified. Even my Dolphin seemed to be smiling his benign assertion of approval. It was a piece of personal arrogance on a grand scale which I was shortly to pay for.

The routine of a ship is a satisfying, pleasurable thing, dictated partly by necessity and partly by choice. I found myself doing things at the same time and in the same way each day although there was no compulsion to do so. The day revolved around the needs of the ship. At dawn I would check round the deck on the look-out for chafe or any sign of wear caused by the constant movement, check the working of the steering vane and its lines to the tiller. I would look round the horizon, read the log, brew my early morning tea and sit in the hatch for ten minutes, listening to the familiar sounds of the ocean, watching the sun gain in power, feeling the warmth of a new day spread through me. I would eat breakfast, wash up, check my vegetables, turning them over and selecting those that should be eaten first. Then I would read for an hour, or listen to music, or embark on some job round the deck or in the cabin.

In the forenoon I would take my morning longitude sights, work them and run my dead reckoning up to noon, ready for a latitude and the ship's position for the day when the sun was on the meridian. Then I would sleep for an hour. At noon the log was read again, the altitude of the sun taken and the position marked with a ringed dot on the chart; the day's run calculated and entered in the log. This was the highspot of the day, the moment when all my feelings, hopes, fears converged like the concentrated beam of a lantern and fixed themselves on that spot on the chart. It was the telltale, the yardstick by which the whole project could be judged.

I learned to keep my eyes on the horizon frequently during the day and the night, scanning the ocean for a ship or any artefact. There is great variety in the ocean. The endlessly repeated waves are all individuals, each accorded by *Iskra* its own special treatment. She would brace herself for each one and then engage it, lifting her bow as she felt its contour under her forefoot, swerving, feinting, shying away or smiting it full face according to the demands of each one, throwing the crystal spray to one side in an expression of exuberant energy and at once engaging the next. They stretched to infinity on all sides, each one a different size, its own unique shape, set at a different angle, containing more or less energy than the others. They varied in colour and in the sound they emitted; some were aggressive, snarling at *Iskra*'s stern like angry dogs as she ran from them, some were placid, rounded, silent; some a deep green or blue, others like slate, dull and opaque.

The sky too, with its strange, even grotesque patterns, was never the same from moment to moment. Sometimes it was all tightly matted with cloud, the sun shining through a hazy ring; sometimes faultlessly clear and blue, or with some grand sweep of a design sailing across its face. In the evenings the sun let go its technicolour fireworks; the world would burst apart with colour as if the very core of the earth had been turned loose along the western horizon. Under the blackness of the night I was the only human creature. I could speak or sing or shout or blaspheme, or marvel aloud at the vastness and wonder of it all and receive no confirmation or rebuttal. I could believe that no other creature existed anywhere except myself. There could be no help for me from any other hand, no encouragement, no confirmation of my existence. There could be no criticism of me, no stricture, no moral reckoning, no rebuke. I set my own standard in all things and kept my own discipline before my God.

Perhaps in the afternoons I would feel the sting of nostalgia and want another person. The afternoons were long - longer than the mornings. I would fall to wondering how I would sustain the next ten, twelve, twenty days alone - an indulgence I could not afford myself. The meanderings of the mind had to be kept in check, or they would lead into unacceptable avenues. I never felt lonely, never wanted to share my magic; it was stronger for being undiluted by another person. Everything belonged to me.

The afternoon was a time for leisure, the only time of the day that consciously needed to be filled. I would eat a light salad lunch, sleep for an hour, and then find occupation - write my journal, make a toy for a child from wood and old pieces of rope, fashion some replacement or modification to the gear, clean a part of the boat that was in need. Usually one job led to another and I became absorbed. I tried not to read in the daytime, reserving this luxury for the hours of darkness. All day and all night I kept an eye on the course, one compass in the centre of the cabin, another on the bridge deck outside. Some days she ran true, never needing adjustment to the vane, others brought small changes in the direction of the trade wind. It tended to back and freshen in the morning and veer at sunset. I knew it instinctively if she strayed from the course. I could feel her if she faltered in her stride or was slewed by a rogue sea catching her under her quarter and nudging her off course. All day and all night I kept an eye on the horizon. I saw nothing.

A hundred years ago the trade wind route was full of shipping; a vessel would expect to see or speak to a ship every few days. Now it is a deserted road. Except for a few yachts and a few ships crossing the route between South Africa and America and Europe, the ocean is empty. I have sailed for weeks and seen nothing. My main meal of the day was in the evening. It was an occasion, carefully planned to suit the ever-diminishing fresh stores, prepared with as much imagination as I could muster and consumed with deliberate, calculated pleasure. After it I would sit in the hatch with my coffee, watch the stars, be entertained by Maestro Mozart's blend of passion with a neat, ordered, view of life, or old grandfather Beethoven thundering and growling into the night, gloomy Brahms or the poignant, doubting melodies of Schubert with his tales of unrequited love. The routine was geared to pass the day calmly, with variety and consciously regulated thoughts to keep the gears of the mind turning smoothly.

The nights at sea are too beautiful, too full of colour and interest, to be spent asleep - too much sleep drugs the mind. Shaw said 'Six hours for a man, seven hours for a woman, eight for a fool.' Food and sleep are both commodities that should be used sparingly if you rely on concentration for your survival. A mind full of sleep and a body full of food are poor watchdogs. There is a balance between fatigue and the sluggish torpor brought on by too much sleep. The mind works efficiently when it has the right amount of sleep, not too much, not too little. People who have had visions or hallucinations or psychic experiences are often insomniacs. I would sleep for an hour in the early part of the night after my meal, for another hour around midnight and again before the dawn when, according to Napoleon, 'A man's courage is at a low ebb'. The full moon was so close and soft that I felt I could reach up and touch it; when new or old it contracted itself to a sliver of silver, hard, remote, mysterious. The stars, fixed in the purple sky, are the wisdom of God. I learned their names and their declinations. Borrowing a morsel of God's wisdom I would fix them with my sextant on the hardening horizon in the first light of morning to calculate *Iskra*'s position on the earth.

I read at night, not about the sea but about the countryside of England, or about the struggles and romances battled out on dry land. I learned poetry by heart - Shakespeare, Keats, Matthew Arnold, Browning and declaimed it into the night or harangued the stars with Shelley or Byron. I sang Mozart arias and Schubert songs; I spewed out ditties and doggerel until the waters shuddered and withdrew into themselves. It was ten days of experience which no person or circumstance can ever take from me, a fraction of life which survives complete in my mind, like a picture.

As if by a signal, when the distance run tipped 1,500 miles on the tenth day, the trade wind began to ease. At first I thought nothing of it. It was a pleasant change for the strain to be slackened. Instead of a mad helter-skelter at seven knots *Iskra* was proceeding with less bluster at five. The anger went out of the seas to be replaced by a more temperate mood. The white crests tumbled over one another with diminished violence, the ocean took on a more placid aspect, the sea a deeper blue, the rolling swells were more tranquil. The tautness went out of the sheets and halyards and guys; the mast no longer strained against shrouds, runners, backstays, the log no longer rotated with such urgent haste. In the first part of the afternoon she kept up five knots, sailing downwind with a restful, timeless roll, the twins nicely rounded, their reefs let free, the steering vane no longer rigid in the wind but gently coaxing *Iskra* to her course. It was rest

after toil, happy relaxation after tension, calm after excitement. By evening the wind was no more than a breeze, the twins hardly filled. By midnight we were becalmed. I looked over the side into the inky sea and there was no forward movement.

There was no wind the next morning. I used the day to good advantage taking down the sails, checking every seam for signs of chafe and stitching where necessary. It was pleasant enough sitting on the hatch in the sun stitching sails and listening to the tape recorder. When one day of calm extended itself into two days I began to be restive. Why had the trade wind died? I pored over the wind chart and read through the weather section of the Atlantic Pilot. There was no mention of calms, *Iskra* was in the trade wind belt - by all the rules she should have a fresh wind from the east. There was not a breath. I took the sails down to save them flogging back and forth as the yacht rolled in the swells. The sea was smooth. The trade wind clouds had gone and in their place was a thin coverlet of grey which the heat of the sun penetrated, but which excluded its bright image. The sky seemed to bear down as if to smother me and *Iskra.* Instead of infinite space the world had come to be a small place, an oppressive place.

On the third day of calm I started the engine and ran it for a day. At first the steady thump of the old diesel heartened me. At least there was movement, the sea was passing by, albeit slowly - perhaps I would move her out of the calm to where there was wind. *Iskra* advanced twenty-eight miles according to sights. Twenty-eight miles in 3,000 - a joke. At this rate I would use all my fuel to no purpose. The engine was meaningless in this ocean, its tiny effort totally irrelevant, the jumping· pistons, the slyly opening valves of no consequence. Without wind I would perish. Surely it was inconceivable that there should not be wind?

Now the time passed like lead; there is no occupation for a man in command of a boat that does not move, no spinning log to record, no sight to work, no alert watch to be kept. With no movement there is no purpose. For the first three days of calm I took sights as usual but now that the dots on the chart were one on top of the next it became a meaningless exercise. The days stretched ahead endlessly. I read but could find no joy, music gave no peace. Close to the surface of my consciousness was a layer of black frustration, anger, resentment. Had the people who wrote books and compiled weather charts ever been in the ocean? Had the pattern of the ocean's weather changed? Was there some devilish intervention, some conspiracy to suspend the trade wind? There was a tedium about it, an overwhelming boredom which I found it impossible to come to terms with.

The dolphins were gone; fair weather friends, deserting me when I needed them. I missed their games - they were a link with the other world I had left behind. I felt aggrieved at their indifference, I had come to rely on them for company; I knew some of them by sight, by their markings and their expressions. I would run to the foredeck when they came and shout my greetings. I always knew when they came by their snorting and splashing - sometimes they rubbed themselves along the bottom of *Iskra*'s hull if I was slow to come to the deck. They would stay for a quarter of an hour, perhaps longer, and then at a signal from their leader they would turn and disappear. Now they left *Iskra* as if she were unclean. The storm petrels were gone too, and the flying fish. It was as if *Iskra* and I had strayed into a cursed enclave of the ocean, shunned by all creatures. I found that I needed these creatures with a desperate urgency. Without them life was an empty mockery. A sailing vessel without wind is without hope or expectation. All the ingenuity, all the tricks that make up the vibrant, alive magic of sail are nothing if the Almighty holds back his breath. I looked at my own Dolphin - now he wore the look of an imbecile, making the world into a joke in bad taste.

I began to swim in the ocean. It was fascinating to see the boat from a distance. I would plunge overboard and swim off as far as I dared. At first I was frightened - I was a tiny piece of matter on the surface of the unknown, an insect, naked and insecure. After a minute I would climb back on board, shaking. Then I swam further off and the next time further, swimming a few strokes and then turning in panic, half expecting the boat not to be there or that a shark had positioned itself between me and *Iskra*. She was a lovely thing, dipping to the ocean swells, shimmering in the sun, with her sails carelessly furled, lying in untidy heaps over the deck. I gazed down into the womb of the ocean, watched the bending shafts of sunlight as they probed downwards, spending their energy in its density, wondered what unknown things might lie in this close darkness.

Sometimes a breeze would come. *Iskra* would move two or three miles and then it would die, leaving her to roll and flog. I trailed a line over the stern, tied a bowline in the end and let myself

I would plunge overboard and swim off as far as I dared

be pulled along, feeling the cool water rush past, looking down into the blue or up at *Iskra* rolling away from me, her sails gently drawing. I let myself back to the bowline, allowing the rope to slip through my fingers until I felt the knot. Then I moved first one hand and then the other across the knot and into the bight, clasped the end of life, holding with my two hands to the last fixed point of my existence. If I let go it would all be over - I would watch her sail away. Why not? I was at a peak of achievement, why not leave now, at the top? Nothing I could do again would equal what I had done. By opening my fingers I could opt out forever, move into another perhaps more profound experience, discover the undiscoverable, solve the unsolvable, learn what can never be learned. Then I was seized by a wild uncontrollable panic. I began to haul myself back along the rope hand over hand. Suddenly she was going faster, the water was drumming in my ears, streaming past like a cataract, pulling and tearing at me; the rope was interminably long, biting into my hands. I found myself under *Iskra*'s stern, found a hold and hauled myself up over the rail and on to the deck. I was shaking, my teeth chattering; I was running salt sweat mixed with the salt sea. I swore never to do that again. I never have.

After a week a breeze came. I sang and shouted with pleasure as *Iskra* began to sail. The twins filled, the bow wave came alive and the yacht began to move towards the west. My elation was brief. By lunchtime the wind had veered to the south so that I had to take in the twins and set the mainsail, then it shifted south-west and by evening it was blowing strongly from the west. This was a cruelty. Now *Iskra* was close hauled, ploughing into a steep head sea laid over the long Atlantic rollers and pointing fifty degrees to the north of her course. Spray swept the deck, sometimes a sea would thunder on board. Life in the cabin was transformed. Instead of the easy trade wind roll that I had become used to, *Iskra* was throwing herself about with malicious violence. Drips forced themselves through the cracks in the coach roof, opened by the weeks of sunshine. Every moveable thing became animated by the motion, strove to get free of its place and find its way to the cabin floor or the lee bunk.

The west wind blew all night, freshening so that I had to reef the mainsail and change to a small jib. *Iskra* began to leak and to ship heavy spray into the cockpit. My depression was complete. How could I have run into this weather in latitude fifteen degrees north, where it had no business to be? So much for a fast passage across the Atlantic. This spell of weather had already put me back more than a week. How long could it go on? I began to get tired and my nerves wore thin. A vicious plunge caught me off balance in the sloping cabin and I slipped and cut my hand on the sharp edge of one of the portholes. It was no more than a scrape but I swore until I had exhausted all the invective I knew. In a rage I smote the porthole with my clenched fist, then I felt ashamed and sat for minutes on the lee bunk reproaching myself and waiting for my heartbeat to return to normal. At daybreak the south-west wind still blew strongly. I put *Iskra* about and headed towards the south-west, still fifty degrees off course, now towards South America.

On the fifth day the wind fell light and then died to nothing. It began to rain, the atmosphere was oppressive and hot. Now the strength of the wind which for days had kept *Iskra* pressed against the contours of the waves, forcing her to follow their undulations with a monotonous rhythm, was released. She rolled and pitched with abandon in a confused sea, the boom swinging wildly and bringing up with a jerk against the sheet, threatening to wrench the blocks out of the deck. I took the mainsail down and lashed it to the boom gallows. This rain might mean a change of weather. I had made no more than a hundred miles in nearly two weeks since the trade wind died. At this rate I would run through my food and water before I reached Antigua.

It rained with tropical intensity until the rain became an upwards extension of the sea itself, with *Iskra* enveloped in a primeval wetness so that she lost the quality of solidity. The rain flowed all over the deck and the coach roof and streamed to waste through the scuppers. I caught it in my cupped hands where it flowed off the furled mainsail and drank deeply. It was fresh and beautiful. I collected it in a can and filled *Iskra*'s tanks. Then it stopped. A breeze came from the east. At first I could not believe it. I checked it with the compass. There was no doubt, there was a breeze, east by north. Already *Iskra*'s bow was paying off towards the west. My depression was transformed. I forgot that I was tired, forgot that I had ever been cast down. In an hour I had set the twin headsails. A watery sun broke through the cloud I had got to know so well and soon the twins were drawing bravely and the boat was leaving behind her a path of gay bubbles. The guy ropes were taut, the sails full of wind and she became once more a happy thing, singing and laughing as she sped towards America. I went to sleep, relaxed and thankful for deliverance.

I woke in an hour. Instinctively I glanced down at the compass clipped to the bunk rail within a foot of my head. *Iskra* was heading east, back on her tracks. At first my consciousness baulked at this information, relayed from the compass card to my brain. This could not be. Had I not set the twins and fixed the course before I went to sleep? Was it a dream? I glanced at the clock and noted that I had been asleep no more than my due time. She must have been taken aback. I went to the hatch, looked aloft and saw that the twins were drawing firmly. Then I looked at the compass again, then went to the master compass under the bridge deck for confirmation. There was no doubt. The wind had swung round through half a circle, taking *Iskra* with it, and was blowing her back towards where she had come from.

I was filled with a white anger. 'You bastard,' I said. With a release of furious energy I jumped out of the hatch and ran for'ard, careless of handholds against the violent rolling, careless of safety harness. 'You bastard,' I muttered again, 'you bastard.' My anger was complete and uncontrollable. It filled my mind and my body like a great wind, was a power inside me over which I had no control; it was as if a spring, wound tight by frustration, had broken the delicate mechanism of my rationality. So bloody *Iskra* was going east instead of west - I would teach her. I flew at the halyards, cast them free and clawed at the sails. They tumbled to the deck in disarray. One of the halyards caught its coil in a half turn and went aloft, far out of reach. As one sail came down, the other fouled a shroud. I swore as I had never sworn, on fire with anger. I tore the hanks from the stays, peeling back a fingernail on the wire so that blood spurted. Blasphemy burst from me as I bundled the sails below, altered the tiller so that *Iskra* swung broadside to the seas and hoisted the mainsail once again, keeping a precarious hold as the boat rolled her gunwales in the confused sea. I caught my bare toe on the pin rail, bruised my knuckle against the iron mast winch; a bare end of rope, animated by the wind, caught me sharply across the chest. The tears streamed down my face but still my anger persisted. At last the mainsail was up, the jib was set and *Iskra* began once again to buck the steep Atlantic seas. I ran back to the cockpit to adjust the steering vane, slipped on the break of the cabin top, fell headlong, hit my head against the end of the tiller and knocked myself out.

I lay unconscious on the cockpit floor, motionless, my head in one corner of the cockpit, one leg doubled under me and the other pointing skywards, like a circus clown in a hilariously contrived act. Then a wave slopped over the weather rail and washed over me.

I became aware of a searing ache in my head, pulled myself up and went below weak and shaking. I looked at my torn hand and was filled with self pity and for the first time, with pain. My head had an angry bump and there was a red scrape down one shin. I bandaged my finger, found myself a glass of Don Felipe's brandy, tried to take stock. I was cornered, forced to look in at myself. For the first time I was lonely, yearning for the company and sympathy of another person, any person man, woman, adult, child - with a despair that was physically painful. Stripped of excuses, self-justifications, I had failed. Faced with a test I had been found wanting. It had been an easy thing for the ocean to upset my small mental world, turning me into an idiot fighting against myself. The balance of the mind is a delicate mechanism if it can be thrown out by a few trivial irritations, each meaningless in itself but together producing a madness that it is impossible to control.

The west wind blew for another night. I sat in the cabin, the oil lamp swinging with *Iskra*'s motion, drawing its sombre shadows across my bruised mind. Sometimes I dozed, sometimes glanced at the compass for some hint of relief. It had all been a failure, a defeat in the ocean inflicted on me by myself, leaving me lonely, my optimism crushed. At dawn the wind fell light again. *Iskra* rolled in the swell like driftwood, without purpose. I looked round the horizon, dejected.

Then I saw it - a ship, not a quarter of a mile distant, steaming towards *Iskra*. She was all white, her name painted in black letters across the side of the bridge - *Centurian*. She was flying the red ensign. She slowed down as she came close alongside; I heard the engine room telegraph and her engines stopped. The captain came to the wing of the bridge with a megaphone. 'You alright?' he shouted. 'Yes,' I replied, 'Fine thanks.' 'Do you require anything?' 'No thanks, I'm fine. On passage to Antigua from La Palma. Will you report me to Lloyds?' 'Certainly. Good luck.' I heard the engine room telegraph again. She gathered her way and was gone. Soon the wind came from the east, strong, steady, purposeful. Inside two days *Iskra* was in English Harbour, Antigua, swinging to her anchor off Nelson's dockyard.

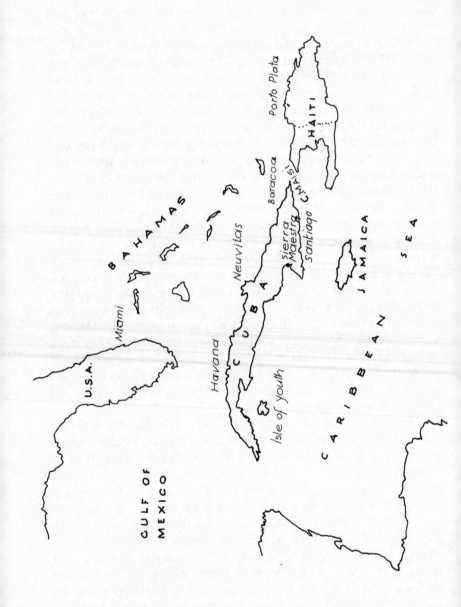

VI

Prisoner

Baracoa lies at the eastern end of the island of Cuba, not more than thirty miles from Cape Maisí, at its tip. It is rugged country, densely forested, steep mountains sheer out of the ocean, few harbours. Columbus landed at Baracoa on his first voyage in 1492. The first Spanish settlement on the island in 1515 was at Baracoa - the remains of the old fortifications are still there. The town is set against the mountains round a crescent beach, a nondescript town with streets of pleasant, unpretentious houses in the Spanish style, baked to pastel shades by the tropic sun, with red tiled roofs, a square, some concrete buildings and the rest *bohios* - the traditional wattle and daub huts which are found all over Cuba and which date back to Indian times. A steep river runs through the town and then alongside the beach, before it flows into the sea. You can bathe in the sea and then rinse yourself in the sweet stream. The Polimita, a land snail with a curious, brightly coloured shell, is unique to this spot.

Coming from the sea the town is beautiful - a smudge of contrast against the vivid mountain. Before Fidel Castro's revolution, Baracoa had no road, its only access was by ship or by light aeroplane. Successive Cuban governments for fifty years had promised to build the road, taxes had been raised, dates fixed, credit taken by politicians. The road never came; always the money melted away in graft, the plans crumbled. Fidel built the road within six years of taking power, with the help of East German and Russian engineers. It is a major civil engineering achievement, winding its dizzy, twisting path to Santiago, Cuba's second city on the opposite coast, over the mountain range, with staggering views of the ocean and the wonderful forest. Every resident of Baracoa is proud of the road.

Iskra arrived unchallenged from the neighbouring island of Hispaniola on the appointed day, at the appointed time, flying her red ensign and her yellow Customs flag. There was a wooden quay out from the shore with a few coasters and fishing boats lying alongside. I anchored behind it and sat in the cockpit looking around and wondering what would happen. I was suffering from toothache which had plagued me for the three day passage from Puerto Plata and I was very tired. The tooth had driven me nearly insane with pain, searing, throbbing, consuming my energy. I had tried to pull it out - with pliers, wrapped in cotton wool, with nylon twine, one end tied round the tooth, the other to the fly wheel of the engine, jerking my head against it but succeeding only in cutting my mouth and breaking the twine. I had found a bottle of oil of cloves in *Iskra*'s medicine chest and this, combined with an overdose of codeine, had eased the pain. I wondered whether there would be a dentist in this town - I wasn't hopeful.

The vaunted sea defences of Cuba, which I had been led to believe would challenge *Iskra* as soon as she entered territorial waters, had not been in evidence. 'They shoot first and ask questions afterwards,' the people at the Cuban Embassy in London had told me, but all I had seen in the approaches to Baracoa and along the coast towards Cape Maisí was a heavily laden coaster whose crew waved cheerfully as I passed. Baracoa, on this afternoon at least, was firmly asleep. With the binoculars I could see a soldier actually sleeping, sitting against the wall of a shed, his legs apart, his head lolling, his rifle propped beside him. An old dog loped along the quay in search of a shady corner, his greying muzzle sniffing the ground, his tail drooping in the dust. As I sat I wondered how it could be that this placid island had been the centre of so much turmoil in the world. After two hours a pulling boat put off from the shore with four soldiers on board, one of them the man I had so recently seen asleep.

I greeted the soldiers in Spanish: 'Buenas tardes, Compeñeros,' and told them that I was expected in Baracoa, that my arrival had been planned for this day. I asked them to go ashore again and inform the Captain of the Port that I had arrived. They went off obediently; I ate an orange and a small piece of biscuit and tried sleep. The voyage from Puerto Plata had been short but rough. As *Iskra* had sailed along the precipitous coast of Haiti with its mountains in a jagged line against a steely blue sky, the wind had freshened. In the Windward Passage between Haiti and Cuba a fierce cross-current whipped up a dangerous sea which crashed on board with destructive force. The toothache started as soon as I left and persisted throughout the passage. My concentration was destroyed by it - *Iskra* was in danger of being swamped but I was concerned only with this pain. If she had foundered it would have been a relief. Now I was exhausted but unable to sleep although the pain, for the time being, had gone.

After two hours the boat came back, this time full of people. They all came on board - a girl dressed in a white coat over her green drill uniform explained that they were a medical delegation. A glass cylinder, like a giant syringe full of yellow liquid, was hoisted up from the boat and placed in the centre of *Iskra*'s cabin. The delegation sat round, a minion operated a hand pump on the cylinder and the girl directed a rubber nozzle which emitted a cloud of some antiseptic vapour into every corner of the accommodation, lockers, drawers, the fo'c'sle, the lavatory. She asked for all my shoes, which were laid out across the cabin floor and given special treatment. 'Higienico' she said knowingly, 'importante para la revolutión.' This task completed she took my blood pressure, tested my heart and pulse and took a sample of blood with another, smaller syringe. She tapped away at the tooth but it lay doggo. The medical delegation went ashore. They had been polite, considerate, serious minded.

The next man to arrive was Teniente Lupez. He came with two soldiers in the same rowing boat; he was wearing a revolver in his belt and an austere, neat uniform. He told me he was a 'functionary of the Party', representing the Ministry of the Interior. He didn't smile. His features were hatchet sharp, brown, like a red Indian's. His speech was curt, he carried his authority with explicit frankness. I told him my story - who I was, why I had come. 'There are no private yachts in Cuba and no facilities for yachting in Baracoa. If a yacht comes here in need of assistance we will help if we can, but she must leave in twenty-four hours. In your case I will have to ask Havana for instructions.' I told him that I had been to Cuba before, was well known and was friendly with people of influence. 'I will telephone Havana and let you know their answer.' He went ashore, leaving the soldiers on board, said he would come back later and take me ashore. He was as good as his word.

We went ashore together in the evening, leaving the soldiers in command and walked through the town to a spacious house in what had been the better class area. It was some sort of headquarters where the senior officials lived, a light, airy, cool place with comfortable cane chairs and potted plants. Lupez said the telephone was out of order but he would contact Havana as soon as he could. He handed me over to David Lobuse. I told David I was feeling ill and wanted to go back on board *Iskra*. He was much younger than Lupez, fat, cheerful, with blue eyes, unusual in Cuba. He took me back through the town to the quay. People gazed at us curiously. We rowed out to *Iskra* in the boat - David wasn't used to boats, I rowed. When we got alongside I said, 'Thank you, David, I'll see you tomorrow when we hear from Havana; now the soldiers can go ashore.' He said, 'No, the soldiers will stay, we put a guard on every ship that comes to Baracoa - regulations.' 'It's not necessary,' I said, 'I can't have two soldiers on my boat - I don't need them, there isn't room.' 'Regulations,' said David, with a disarming smile. 'They're nice boys.' I lay sweating in my bunk all night, listening to the low chatter of the soldiers, to the bumps and bangs as the rowing boat came back at the change of their watch and the clump of heavy boots on *Iskra*'s clean decks.

I felt bitter, depressed, ill the next morning. 'What are they guarding?' I ask in my daily journal, 'Me or *Iskra*? Why guard me, when I don't want it? Are they trying to prevent me from going ashore? Trying to keep me from meeting anyone?' I invited the soldiers inside out of the sun, gave them cups of coffee, which they seemed to have a poor opinion of, bars of chocolate. One of them ate the chocolate as if he had never tasted such a thing in his life, the other looked at the label carefully and then put it in his hat. 'Para los niños,' he said - for the children. Lupez came later in the morning. 'I have telephoned to Havana; the reply will come in due time.' I attacked him about the soldiers. 'I can't have soldiers in my boat - there's no room - it's not necessary - I am a friend of Cuba, not an enemy.' He was firm, detached. 'The guards must stay - it's the regulations.'

I went ashore with him, walked up through the town to the big house and sat down to a meal of rice and meat prepared by an old cook who bustled in out of the kitchen to make sure his patrons, or his masters, whatever they might be, were enjoying their meal. There were five of us; two officers, a civilian, Lupez and me - no women. I could eat nothing. 'When I was in Cuba before,' I said, 'no guard was put on my boat.' 'This is Baracoa, not Havana,' Lupez said. 'Wait till we hear from the Ministry.' Half-way through the meal David came in. 'You don't look well,' he said. I told him about the toothache, the bad weather in the Windward Passage, that the soldiers had kept me awake. I said I wanted to send a cable to England to tell them I was safe, to change some money, buy stores. David said, 'When the permission comes from Havana. Lie down for an hour - you'll feel better.' He took me into a cool room off the tiled patio with shutters against the midday sun, a mosquito net over a bed with clean sheets. I went to sleep at once and woke when the evening was giving way to night.

When I came out into the patio David and Lupez were sitting in the cane chairs conversing. I joined them. The cook brought tiny cups of strong, sweet black coffee on a silver tray. I told them again about *Girl Stella*'s voyage to Cuba, how we had been well received and had sailed from Santiago along the south of the island, round Cape San Antonio at the opposite end to where we were now; mentioned people I had met who were well known - artists, writers, even a minister who had been to visit *Girl Stella*. I told them about articles I had written in the Cuban magazine Bohemia about *Girl Stella*'s voyage. I could see they were impressed, even Lupez was softening. 'You must take the guards off,' I said, 'I can't live in this way.' I told them I wanted to telephone my friends in Havana, asked whether there was a dentist in the town. 'I'll take you to the clinic tomorrow.' David said. I had no fresh food - no eggs, no bread, no fruit, no money to buy these things unless they would allow me to change a traveller's cheque or change my US dollars. 'Wait until the call comes from Havana,' Lupez said.

I could see his dilemma - he was caught by his own bureaucracy. If he made me leave, as he had every right to do, it might turn out that I was, as I said, a semi-official guest with proper permission for my visit. He would be in trouble. If he let me stay and move about freely he could equally be in trouble. I might turn out to be a journalist at best, or some sort of spy or infiltrator anxious to stir up trouble. He had decided to keep me under close watch, not a prisoner but not free either; keep me happy so that if I turned out to be a person of influence I would have no reason to do him any mischief. He must have cursed the bureaucracy which worked so slowly and painfully that it would take days or weeks to get an answer to a simple question. It was a tight-rope for him as well as for me. Before David took me back to *Iskra* the two of them went into another room and I heard earnest conversation. When I went on board with David the soldiers both went ashore with him. He looked hard at me, smiled with a suspicion of a wink. 'I'll come for you early in the morning and we'll go to the clinic.' he said. I slept happily in my solitude.

Baracoa was unlike any other town in the Caribbean. There were no gay shop windows, no open bars, no advertisements, no neon lights, no cars, no busy crowds. On the surface it seemed asleep yet things were going on underneath. 'Everyone is at work.' David said. As we walked to the clinic we passed groups of people working on a building site; we passed a school full of the earnest hum of children, the new hospital, a bright, cheerful place with the patients sitting on a long cool verandah. The town looked run-down and poor but there were no begging children, no policemen; it was unpainted but clean. The dental clinic was efficient. My tooth had an abcess under it - a Cuban dentist extracted it. His drill came from Czechoslovakia, his dental chair from Hungary, the metal instrument cabinet from East Germany. 'There was no dentist here before,' he said, "Now there are three.' 'Before' always meant 'before the revolution'. I felt a relief from nagging pain once the tooth was gone. I had been to a dentist in Tortola; he had made a filling which the Cuban dentist showed me was a perfunctory job and had charged $20. 'No one pays for medical treatment here.' he said. They were all proud of their revolution, at least to an outsider. After lunch in the big house David took me back on board. There had been no telephone call from Havana. 'When the swelling goes from my face and I begin to feel better', I thought, 'I'll start making a fuss.'

I spent six days in Baracoa waiting for the telephone message from Havana. It occurred to me that I was free to leave at any time. I could have slipped out of the port at night, or even in the daytime; I doubted whether anyone could have stopped me even if they had wished to. It would have been a short and easy journey to the Bahamas and there was no reason to believe that the Cubans would have tried to stop me - indeed the power to do so was not in evidence. Lupez had asked me for my passport and the ship's papers, which I had given him, and this would make it awkward for me to leave clandestinely. I never went ashore without David, or another soldier called Fernando who sometimes came out in the boat to collect me from *Iskra*. I could have inflated my rubber dinghy or moved alongside the quay but I refrained. I knew they would prefer to have me somewhere they could keep tabs on me; I was either ashore with David or on board and this suited them. If I was going to visit Cuba, I decided, I would have to play the game their way. I understood the hatchet-faced Lupez's point of view. I had no money and was never taken near the Bank, I spent hours on the telephone in the big house trying to call Havana but could never get through.

I made such a fuss about sending cables that in the end David took me to the old Cable & Wireless office, which still existed in the town and I went through the formality of cabling Lechuga, one of my friends in Havana who was the Cuban minister to the UN and whom I had told about my voyage in *Iskra*. I cabled Celia, at home, to tell her I was at least safe. Neither of the cables ever arrived. The cable to Lechuga read: "Arrived Baracoa 30th. Waiting permission to visit Havana. Can you help?" I had no money but everything I needed was given to me: the old cook in the big house gave me bread and eggs and a few fresh vegetables when he had them. I had most of my meals with Lupez and David and any odd soldier or itinerant official who might be staying there. Soon I began to get on well with David, a compassionate, affable man who sympathised with my plight; even the austere Lupez began to soften but he would not relax his vigilance over me. I was never left alone for a single moment.

David had the use of a jeep and he took me around the countryside in this remote eastern tip of Cuba. We went over the new road, the loveliest journey I have ever made by road, beating for scenery anything I have seen in the Azores or the Canaries or

wild mountain ranges, all blue and green and pale brown

Spain, even more spectacular than the road round the end of the Sogne Fiord in Norway and that between Sao Paulo and Santos in Brazil. It soars into the remote, green hazy interior, snaking upwards round the mountain sides, sometimes glued to the vertical rock face, sometimes plunging into valleys and over gorged rivers, or across on concrete stilts from one dizzy height to the next. It offers views of wild mountain ranges, all blue and green and pale brown, of lush clefts dropping sheer from the roadside and at its peak, of the ocean on both sides of the island - the Caribbean to the south, the Old Bahama Channel to the north. It is a major engineering work, graced with its own beauty as is sometimes true of the great works of man.

David took me through remote mountain tracks to villages deep in the forest, showed me schools in the country where there had been no school before, new agriculture with a market for the first time, new hope where there had been none. In the countryside Fidel's revolution was at its best and David was its best exponent. He knew and was on good terms with everyone, was liked and respected by all sides. He seemed to know everyone by their Christian names and knew all about their troubles and aspirations. He was a man tailor-made for leadership in a society that needed wise leaders.

Every day I nagged about the message from Havana and every day some excuse was found. Someone was coming over to see me from Santiago, or the telephone lines were out of order, or someone was coming to interview me from Havana but couldn't get a flight. I began to believe that a decision was being taken at a high level, that they would prefer me to leave but couldn't think of a way of achieving this without offending protocol or ordinary good manners. Cubans, like Spaniards, are always anxious to act correctly. Whenever I asked to change money or to telephone or to send a cable it was 'Not until the telephone call comes from Havana.' or 'Wait till the Compañero comes from Santiago'. David filled in my days as best he could. He took me to see day nurseries, the hospital, schools, or into the country where we talked with dozens of people he knew who all told me that everything in their lives was fine since the revolution, which was clearly true in some respects at least. Cuba had been a sad place of graft and vicious exploitation under the dictatorship of Batista.

We went to an old people's home where the inmates were sitting out on the verandah drinking fresh, cold milk - unheard of before except for the well-off. David was immensely proud of this novelty, offering it as proof of the revolution's compassion. I asked a fine old gentleman, who was a picture of content whether things were better now or before the revolution. 'Much worse now,' he said firmly, 'there's no liberty.' Freedom, clearly, is what you think of it. A man who believes he is free, is free; a man who believes he is not is a slave.

After a week, Lupez came striding into the house where I was trying, vainly, to get through to Havana on the telephone and said, 'Be ready in half an hour - you're going to Havana.' I had anticipated something of this sort and *Iskra* was ready to be left. David took me on board, Fernando undertook to watch over her and put out extra lines if it came on to blow a *Norte*. I packed my bag from a list I had ready, fastened a canvas cover over *Iskra's* cockpit and we hurried to the tiny airport tucked in under the mountain. The plane left three hours later and took us across the mountains to Santiago where we were met by a man called Danio in an ancient, beat-up Cadillac with a clapped-out exhaust. Danio had driven the 1,000 kilometres from Havana, nursing the old car from one garage to the next and taking three days to make the journey. Lupez had been telling the truth about the man from Havana.

Nothing was said about paying; I was given no bill for my two day stay in the Hotel Versailles in Santiago, the best hotel in Cuba, while Danio's old motor car was patched up for the return drive. From this I assumed I was the guest of the Revolution, although no one put it to me in this way. During my week in Baracoa I had got used to living without money - it was a welcome change. Everything I wanted I asked for and my demands were simple. There were no consumer goods in shops - nothing to buy, not even a picture postcard. Food and clothing and what consumer goods existed were distributed to the people through co-operatives and a centralised distribution organisation. The old shops were boarded up or used for other purposes, making the towns look drab and depressing. The American blockade had stripped Cuba of the trappings of civilisation. Now every door handle, every lavatory seat, every window latch, every tin of floor polish had either to be made on the island or imported 3,000 miles across the ocean.

Danio's old Cadillac was held together with bits of string, or wire for permanent repairs, or anything that would serve except chewing gum, which was unobtainable. Transport was one of Cuba's key problems. No motor cars or spares had been imported from America since the blockade; those that had survived were in a state of acute decrepitude. We drove to Havana without stopping except for petrol and periodic inspections of the massive engine, head shakings and attempts to stop leaking exhaust fumes and leaking water from the radiator. We drove through beautiful countryside to the north of the Sierra Maestra, and along the central highway to Bayamo, Holguin, Camaguey, Sancti Spiritu and Veradero for coffee at day-break. After a day's non-stop driving we pulled up outside the Deauville Hotel on Havana's Malecon, with the ocean across the road and the city behind.

According to Saint Matthew, 'A prophet is not without honour, save in his own country.' The Cubans at least were astonished that I should have retraced my steps after losing *Girl Stella* and they were pleased that I should want to come back to Cuba. I was besieged by journalists anxious to write articles about *Iskra*'s voyage, which they did with varying degrees of accuracy. Lechuga himself came to see me in the hotel, with his daughter Lilian who was a journalist on Bohemia magazine. I wrote an article myself for Bohemia and articles appeared daily in every Cuban newspaper and periodical. I was famous, all doors were opened for me. I became known as 'El navigante solitario'; I made broadcasts on Cuban radio and plans were made for a television film to be made in Veradero on what was to be *Iskra*'s triumphal progress from Baracoa to Havana. I was allocated a young man called Manuel, with another decaying Cadillac, to look after me during my stay and to provide for all my wants. I had only to ask to receive the best seats for the ballet, a reservation in the best restaurant in Havana, a visit to the fabulous nightclub 'La Tropicana'. I was given a special press card with a photograph of myself officially stamped by the Ministry which gained me entry anywhere. I was ushered to the front of every queue for every scarce commodity or entertainment or privilege. I could go to the diplomatic shop to buy anything I needed in the way of stores.

For a time I was pleased and flattered by this astonishing elevation from the ranks of ordinary mortals. I saw my friends from my previous visit, was invited out every night, was wined and dined and breakfasted to the limit of Cuba's austere regime. One day an old friend, Bolaños, back in Cuba from the embassy in London where I had met him, telephoned me in the hotel and invited me to go with him to cut cane - an honour above all honours. No man can do more for another man than this. One day, remembering La Palma for a fleeting instant, I telephoned Dolores's little sister. I went to her house in Miramar, once Havana's smartest suburb. Lourdes was dark, beautiful, intelligent, unattached. The gold locket sat sweetly on her bosom. She offered food, drink, comfort to a hungry, thirsty, lonely sailor.

This ascent to the stars had been no part of my plan. I had intended, and had agreed with the Cuban Embassy in London, to go to Baracoa and get clearance to call at half-a-dozen ports along the north coast of Cuba towards Havana, taking my own time, picking my weather, paying my own expenses, as we had during *Girl Stella*'s voyage, and arriving in Havana with perhaps a month in hand to get *Iskra* ready for the return voyage to England. Instead, I had been made into a celebrity which would make it more difficult to see the country as I wanted to see it. I have always found that cruising in a small boat is a good method of getting to know a foreign land. A man who arrives in a boat is immediately a part of the place, is immediately accepted by the local people. He has sailed across an ocean to make his visit, an earnest of his desire to learn something about the country and this gives him a special standing. He is distinct from a tourist or an official visitor who falls into a set category and is treated in a set way by people specially designated to cater for him. In foreign parts I meet people who ask me to their homes, talk to me, exchange their ideas with mine and whose hospitality I can return on board *Iskra*.

I knew that being a guest of the Cuban government would destroy this relationship but there was nothing I could do - I must take things as they came or go away. The Cubans were used to foreign delegations. They were ready to show off their country's undisputed achievements with genuine pride but they only showed what they wished to be seen. Manuel, as it turned out, was an unlucky choice as my guide. He was young, ambitious, a born opportunist who had learned how to use the system to his own advantage with cynical disregard for principle. He was concerned above all else with his own comfort, safety and well-being. I tried but found it hard to respect him. To my dismay, I was told at the Ministry that because I was alone and the coast was dangerous, Manuel was to come with me on board *Iskra* for the voyage to Havana. I believe he was as dismayed as I. This would make it easier for me, they said, although they did not tell me how.

Havana was a city of charm and character. Lourdes showed me round, took me to the old quarter, round the cathedral where she had friends who lived along narrow alleys, through bowery arches, up cool stone steps among the red tiles and shaded balconies of the old city. We argued far into the night over bottles of rum purchased from the diplomatic shop; the Cubans never tired of arguing the merits and demerits of their revolution, all they needed was the rum, which was strictly rationed. Between us, our friends numbered writers, painters, journalists, government bureaucrats, factory workers - Lourdes herself was a professor of geography in Havana University. Everyone in Cuba argued - without restraint as far as I could judge.

The city was a calm place with few cars but many buses, always crammed and racing through the traffic-free streets at breakneck speed. The bars and most of the shops were closed, the city needed a coat of paint, there were holes in the road. Yet it had an atmosphere of hope and optimism, a kind of run-down determination as if its glories would one day be restored to it. It was a nicer city than it had been when Batista ruled. Having lost its glitter, its vice, its gambling, its crime , it had become law-abiding, decent, safe.

Plans were made for my stay in Cuba. I was to go back to Santiago, make a rapid tour of the Sierra Maestra in a jeep, accompanied by Manuel, then return to *Iskra* in Baracoa and after a visit to the remote eastern tip of Cuba, set sail for Nuevitas, Caibarien, Isabella de Sagua, Vardero and finally Havana. I would have liked to have called at more ports along the coast - Puerto Padre, or Bahia de Nipe. Lourdes was a native of Puerto Padre; she said she might be able to come and meet me there for a few days. This was refused, for no reason that I could understand. The passage would take me until the end of February; I would spend a month fitting out in Havana and then sail direct for Bermuda. I believed I might not be welcome in Florida or any part of the USA after a long stay in Cuba. It would be better to sail direct to Bermuda to avoid complications with the US immigration authorities.

After a week in Havana I caught the plane back to Santiago. The jeep did not materialise. The greatest Cuban failing, a national characteristic, is to make promises, often unsolicited, which they have not the means to carry out. There was a joke among Havanan diplomats: Russians say 'no' when they mean 'yes'; the Cubans say 'yes' when they mean 'no'. We waited in the Hotel Versailles for three days until Manuel secured another old Cadillac and we set out for the Sierra Maestra, the romantic heartland of Cuba's revolution. I had a strong desire to explore the Sierra. In *Girl Stella* we had been to Chivirico on the coast where the mountains drop sheer into the sea. I wanted to go across the mountains to Minas de Frio which had been Che Guevara's headquarters during the revolutionary war.

The revolution was born in the Sierra, a range of rugged country extending along the south of the island from Santiago to Cape Cruz. The highest mountain, Turquino, is 6578 feet. On December 2nd 1956 Fidel Castro arrived from Mexico in an old motor yacht called Granma, with eighty-two ex-patriot revolutionaries on board, one of whom was the Argentinian doctor Che Guevara. They came with the intention of overthrowing the regime of Fulgenio Batista, a regime supported by a modern army of 30,000 equipped and financed from America. Off the fishing village of Belis, the Granma went aground. The rebel soldiers abandoned her, wading to the shore through a mangrove swamp and leaving their equipment and supplies behind. The force was spotted by Batista's planes, ambushed in a cane field at Alegría de Pio and cut to pieces. Twelve survivors made their way to the Sierra and from this beginning the Cuban revolution grew to maturity and then victory. Painstakingly they built a force of peasants and political dissidents into an army, their numbers swelled each week by opponents of the dictatorship and defecting soldiers. Within two years they broke out of the Sierra, spread over Cuba, gaining in strength as they inflicted defeat after defeat on a hated and despised tyranny. When Castro's, Guevera's and Camilio Cienfuegos' rebel columns marched into Havana on January 2nd 1959 they opened a new era in Latin American, even world, history.

Manuel's Cadillac was a second best. I had wanted to go through the Sierra on foot, hitch-hiking if no jeep could be found, and cross over the mountains from Chivirico to Minas. Manuel would have none of this plan, walking and hitch-hiking were not in his programme. Minas is at the top of the mountain range with majestic views to the sea on either side of Cuba. It was Che Guevara's headquarters during the first part of the revolutionary war - the crude peasant's hut he lived and worked in is still there.

A bohío in the Sierra Maestra

El Che, as he is still called, created the philosophy which powered the revolution; now he has become its foremost saint. A school town has been built in Minas. We had to walk for four hours to get there, toiling up the mountain side in the heat. All the building materials for the school were manhandled up the mountain.

Cuba was full of projects like the school city in the Sierra Maestra. There was a new town built in remote, wild mountains at La Gran Tierra, where there was another boarding school. There were more of them in Pinar del Río, the western province of Cuba, and the Isle of Pines in the south, has been re-named Isle of Youth and been made into a school with agricultural projects worked by the children. There were schools for Cuba's friends in the Communist bloc - children from Nicaragua, from Ethiopia and from half a dozen black African countries had their own schools and were taught by Cubans. Everybody went to school in Cuba, the ideal of education being basic to the new philosophy; illiteracy, which used to affect between forty and fifty per cent of the population has been brought down to something below five per cent. Education was regarded as the most potent weapon in the revolution's calendar.

I was beginning to worry about my Dolphin. A strong *norte* blew up while Manuel and I were in Santiago; I could feel the wind screaming round the Hotel Versailles. I had left *Iskra* with a line to a mooring buoy as well as to her anchor and I had made Fernando swear he would keep a close watch on her.

I had remembered as the plane had flown out of Baracoa, across the mountains, that I had left some fresh vegetables and fruit in a locker and I had asked David to go on board and clear them out or they would rot. I wondered how my Dolphin felt about being left alone for all this time in an alien country. I had been away for nearly three weeks, had driven the whole length of Cuba with Danio and flown back with Manuel. I had been into the Sierra to Minas de Frio and to Los Colorados in the swamps where the Granma' invasion had landed.

David met us in Santiago. He had managed to beg or borrow a jeep and we drove through the rough mountain country to the light house on Cape Maisí, surely the remotest place on earth. The road was often no more than a track cut from the forest, splashing through rivers, forcing us to ascend near vertically in low ratio across the intricate relief of the jumbled up mountain mass, some of it hardly explored. La Gran Tierra had been a tiny village, now its population had been quadrupled - it had a school, a hospital a generating plant and a water supply. We spent a night in an austere guest house in La Gran Tierra, the bed as hard as stone and then drove back to Baracoa across the road of La Farola. I saw *Iskra* as we came down the hill into the town, lying peacefully to her buoy as I had left her. Fernando had doubled her lines.

Manuel, by making representations in the proper quarter, managed to extricate himself from the necessity of sailing in a small boat. One look at *Iskra* was enough to convince him that a life on the ocean was not for him. 'I can't swim', he said, 'and I shall be sick'. I congratulated him on his good sense. Instead, he was to follow *Iskra* around from port to port in the Cadillac - a waste of resources I protested, Cuba's oil is carried 4,000 miles from the Black Sea. In his place, I was to have a young man called Jorge. I protested again that I had sailed many miles by myself and thought I would manage the odd 500 to Havana but Lupez insisted, on orders from Havana. 'Jorge will help you,' he said. I doubted this confident assertion but agreed to take him. Perhaps they still thought I was a spy - Cubans are paranoid about spies, rather as the English are but perhaps with more justification. They like to keep tabs on their visitors, and with the CIA working full time to undermine their regime it was not surprising.

Jorge and I embarked and set sail for Nuevitas which is 200 miles to the west. He was a nice lad, although I would not have gone out of my way to choose him as a companion on what might be a difficult voyage along a coast strewn with off-lying dangers, poorly marked, inadequately charted and largely unlit. He had once been fishing he told me, and was sure he wouldn't be seasick. Jorge was a child of the revolution, he had never known the fleshpots of capitalism. He was fascinated with what he found on board *Iskra,*: tins and packets of food he examined with minute interest, marvelling how they were printed in two, sometimes three colours. He learned how to light the gas stove with studied concentration, he approached the lavatory pumps and valves as if they were machines of the highest technology. He had never cooked anything in his life and had no notion of putting things away in their place. He was used to a world where women did all the domestic work. He ate prodigiously until I feared for my stores which I knew would be difficult to replace. Tins of tuna fish, cheese, marmalade and chocolate disappeared in astonishing quantities. I believe he was frightened, as many Cubans are frightened of the sea. He wanted to play the radio all day at full volume. Whenever I insisted on switching it off he would sing between his teeth some Cuban doggerel to the unlikely tune of 'Auld Lang Syne', slightly off key.

At first there was a light westerly wind and *Iskra* sailed calmly along this beautiful, frightening coastline; beautiful in the green mountains, like the painted curtain of an exotic opera, dropping sheer into the sea, frightening in its inhospitability - no fringe of forgiving sand, no haven, no relief or refuge against an angry ocean. I taught Jorge to steer but found that he could not be alone without waking me on some pretext and could not concentrate for more than a few minutes. At night the wind dropped away to nothing. I took *Iskra* off shore a few miles, dropped the sails and went to sleep. The next day a lovely breeze came from the north-east and she bowled past this astonishing coast at her best speed.

I began to like Jorge. His values were fixed for him and it never occurred to him to question them. He had no misgivings about the regime he lived under, accepting its discipline and its philosophy without question. Having no culture and no cause to think deeply, he was free of responsibility. He laughed easily, was kind and I believe completely honest. He took a passionate liking to my Breton fisherman's hat which I had bought years previously in Concarneau, and wore it all the time, even when he was asleep, which was a good proportion of his time.

We passed Cape Leontin in the afternoon and at night the wind died again. That night the sky had a thick, heavy look about it and the barometer went up sharply - sure sign of a *norte*. I slept for as long as I could against what I knew would happen and at dawn, sure enough, the wind went to the south-west, then north-west, then north, freshening hour by hour. *Iskra* passed through her catalogue of sail changes - one reef, small staysail, two reefs, three reefs, small jib and finally, storm trysail and reefed staysail. The seas in the Old Bahama Channel were short and steep. They thundered across the foredeck as she furrowed through them. Jorge's belongings fell to the lee side, he followed them, to occupy the comfortable lee bunk with a bucket secured beside him. He began to moan softly. As we passed Porto Padre he saw the lights to lee'ard. 'Go in,' he said, 'I'm dying - put in at once.' When we arrived at Nuevitas he was ashore before the ropes were fast, with my hat at a jaunty angle. I never saw him again, or the hat and there was no further mention of a crew for *Iskra*.

The discipline of the Cuban revolution is formidable. Lourdes' son went to Poland to do a three-year degree course in port engineering as part of the development of the Cuban merchant marine. He came back shocked at the apparent looseness of moral values in Poland, the lack of *conciencia*, a word of special significance in Cuba, meaning 'commitment to the revolution' or 'scrupulousness'. 'Tiene conciencia este joben' is more than a compliment, it is a term of deep respect, meaning that the young man has a correct attitude towards the revolution and is aware of his obligations to it. People who have this *conciencia* are happy in Cuba - they fit into the machine, thrive on it, benefit from it. They have found something outside themselves to struggle for, a principle they are happy to fight for through their work and morality. They spend their holidays in voluntary labour cutting sugar cane, regulate their lives strictly within close, even old-fashioned precepts of what is permissible and what is not. It is like Victorian England with the fire of the kibbutz under it. Those who are outside this huge fraternity of conformity are miserable. Sometimes they came on board *Iskra*, young and old, begging me to hide them in some corner of the boat and take them out of Cuba.

Like all fanatical believers those with *conciencia* are intolerant. Non-believers are despised and treated with contumely, harassed, though not persecuted. The majority are in many respects better off now than they were before, which is the strength of the revolution. I was able to see this clearly from *Iskra* as I progressed from one small place to another, gaining a view of Cuba that is never seen by tourists or official visitors. The degree of betterment seems to depend greatly on the individual who was in command, the local party functionary - whether he was like David with his humour, his easy familiarity and his compassion, or like Lupez of the hatchet face. There was no deep poverty, no squalor, no shanty towns, no children without shoes.

It was a strange progress. Always Manuel was there to meet me in the old Cadillac with a programme of visits. I saw schools and nurseries and hospitals, cement factories, sugar refineries or *centrales* as they are called. I went to village meetings where 'top workers' were elected to be trained for membership of the Communist party, to a fishing co-operative which had exceeded its target and was celebrating with great energy. I went on board a big merchant ship and lunched in a communal dining room with the Captain, a young man of twenty-four. I was serenaded by a group of *Pioneros*, a kind of political wolf cub and brownie organisation, who had composed a song in honour of *Iskra*. I was interviewed and photographed by every newspaper along the coast; I gave press conferences, a television film was made of *Iskra*, which only came out in bits because the cameras were ancient and didn't work properly. I took part in a sailing regatta of 'Snipe' dinghies, being saved from last place by a young man on day release from a mental hospital. I entertained a group of ladies from the Communist Brigade, all armed with revolvers which they left in a pile in *Iskra*'s cockpit out of fraternal consideration.

The *nortes* seemed to follow me along the coast. From Nuevitas to Caibarien it blew force 8; my chart was hopelessly inadequate and I got in by luck rather than judgement. The local fishermen were astonished that *Iskra* had survived the gale which they told me had been registered at force 10 on the Beaufort scale. They offered to mend my torn jib if I could find them the nylon thread. When I arrived, Manuel was on the quay with the next instalment of my programme. Unaware that I was exhausted and needed sleep above all else, he would drag me off in the old Cadillac to meetings, dinner parties, press interviews, where I couldn't keep my eyes open.

A pilot took *Iskra* inside the reef from Caibarien to Isabella, a gnarled, weathered old sailor who knew every cut and shallow among the mangrove islands. We wound a tortuous route through the cays where alligators flopped into the water, across shallows with inches under *Iskra*'s keel, past remote settlements where before the revolution people had never seen a school or heard of a hospital. On this passage and for the remainder of the voyage to Havana, *Iskra* was escorted by a small ship of the Cuban navy, sporting two guns and a crew of eighteen. Manuel and a chauffeur trundled along the coast in the old Cadillac to alert the local dignitaries and the population and to meet me when *Iskra* arrived. I got very tired of being a celebrity. I began to crave for Bradwell Creek and a pint of bitter in the Green Man. My Dolphin wore a bemused look.

Iskra arrived in Havana towards the end of February. Miraculously, she and I were both unscathed after a harrowing voyage. Sailing alone along a coast, even a sympathetic coast with good harbours and accurate charts,is not easy. This Cuban coast in the winter was a nightmare, made a thousand times worse by the attentions of Manuel. It wasn't his fault. His job was to extract the maximum of publicity and at the same time to demonstrate to me the manysided marvels of the revolution so that I could go home afterwards and write about them. It was also his job to keep a close eye on me. I made the foolish mistake of allowing him to find out about my attachment to Lourdes, which he immediately relayed back to his boss at the Ministry.

Having made a substantial investment in my visit it was natural that the authorities should want something out of it. All the same, I believe the Cubans took trouble over *Iskra* and me because our voyage captivated their imaginations. First, they thought it a fine thing that I should want to visit Cuba in the *Girl Stella* and to make some attempt to discover the truth about Castro's revolution through the welter of propaganda. Secondly, they were pleased that having lost *Girl Stella* I should want to come back again. The operation would have been more successful if I had been given a more compatible and a more adventurous companion who could have come with me on board *Iskra*. This would have been an invaluable help to me and would have made for a more fruitful visit.

I know I can never make another voyage to Cuba in *Iskra*, or any other yacht. The flair and initiative that allowed those first officials to let *Girl Stella* into the country, and which led to this voyage, could never happen again. Now the system has become tight and disciplined and conformist and inward-looking - there is no room any more for imagination and creative thinking. The warriors of the cold war were tight-lipped hard men, like Lupez of the hatchet face.

Iskra arrived off the city of Havana before dawn on a cloudless morning. My escort entered the harbour at the Moro Castle, leaving me to drift on a faint breeze past the frontage of the city to the Rio Almandarez, marked by a stone tower with a red light, where *Girl Stella* had been berthed. The silent city was slowly waking itself; I heard a cracked bugle call from the old fort, saw a flag hoisted to the truck of the signal mast. An early bus crawled along the Malecon like a glow worm, the tall buildings took their shape, standing together like business men in earnest conversation. I could see the Havana Libre hotel, which was once the Hilton, with a light on its peak; the radio station, the hospital, the pink but faded grandeur of the Hotel Nationale, my room in the Versailles and further to the west the end of Lourdes' road in Miramar. I took down the sails and motored into the Rio Almandarez, blowing *Iskra*'s hooter so that the bridge keeper stopped the traffic and opened the old iron bridge. By the time I had berthed alongside the boat yard everyone was awake and at work.

The manager of the yard, Arturo, was the same as had welcomed *Girl Stella* - it was like coming home. I would stay in Havana for over a month, getting ready for the voyage home, discovering the scents of a new city and a new relationship which I knew, deep down, could have no permanence. I wanted to spend a week in the cane fields before I left. Cutting cane is a religious rite, a homage, in Cuba. I believed I could not know the country until I had done it - like falling in love in a foreign country in order to learn the language. I mentioned cane cutting to Manuel and saw the hunted look come into his eyes - this was something he would somehow avoid. *Iskra* was besieged in

Havana. People came on board in a stream so that I found it hard to get my work done. I was invited all over the city. In my odd times I would walk over the iron bridge and visit Lourdes' cool garden in Miramar.

VII

The Cane Fields

Martinez Prieto had been a trade union leader in Batista days. He had been an opponent of the dictatorship, had organised strikes. He had been run to earth, tortured and murdered by Batista's secret police. Now a sugar *centrale* in the cane fields near Havana is named after him. The Centrale Martinez Prieto was where I went with Brigade 37 to cut cane. At eight in the morning the lorry arrived at the boatyard and I climbed up over the tailboard to join a dozen men in straw hats and jeans, laughing and joking like schoolboys on a jaunt. Manuel had done his work well. Because I speak Spanish he had been able to arrange for me to go cane cutting with a Cuban brigade - I would be treated as any Cuban, not as a foreign celebrity. Bolaños' invitation had come to nothing, like so many gestures, but I wasn't sorry. With him I would have joined a diplomatic brigade reserved for foreigners, which I knew would have been something of a propaganda exercise. I had asked Manuel to use his considerable ability as a 'fixer' and he had come up with Brigade 37. 'It'll be hard work.' he said ruefully.

The *centrale* dominates the skyline, towering out of the acres of cane like a mechanical juggernaut to which the voluntary *macheteros* sacrifice their toil in every *zafra*, the Spanish word for the sugar cane harvest. The tall chimney belches smoke into the crisp sky, the machinery snorts and pants as it takes in the cane, the grinding wheels crush and squeeze, a thick river of liquid flows through the intestines of the *centrale* and emerges in a cascade of rich, brown sugar. It is a satisfying process, something that can be understood and appreciated, that fascinates without bewildering. Cane in at one end, sugar out at the other.

The buildings of the *campamento* are long low huts with concrete floors and corrugated roofs, each with iron-framed bunks in a double tier, each bunk enclosed by a mosquito net, each with one coarse unbleached sheet and one blanket. There was no other furniture. The *macheteros* had suitcases, wooden boxes or kit bags. They each found themselves a square foot of floor space which they claimed as their own. There was one hut with a row of showers, another with a long washing trough where four or five taps could sometimes be persuaded to give forth a trickle of water, and another with a row of earth latrines. One of the huts contained the office of the *campamento*, a small barber's shop and a library. The dining hut, with the kitchens beside it, had rows of concrete benches set at concrete tables. At one end was a notice board showing details of the *zafra*, the amount of cane cut to date, the amount short or in excess of the target and the percentage sugar yield. There was another board with a poster of Che Guevara and notices about the routine of the *campamento*. The dining hut was open on three sides. The *campamento* was built on a slight rise and from it I could look out across miles of country, miles of cane - cane as far as the eye could reach, broken only by occasional clumps of royal palms, waving their heads in the breeze like savages. On one side a single track railway cut through the cane towards distant hills. At dawn the sun would rise out of the cane in front of the hut, at sunset it would sink into the cane behind.

Brigade 37 arrived at the *campamento* in several lorries which brought them from various points in Havana. They had been on leave for two days after thirteen days of work and they would stay for another thirteen days until they saw their homes again. Some had not been home - those who lived so far away that the return journey, in two days, was not practicable. Pedrito ticked them off his list as they arrived. They spent the afternoon settling in, gossiping, exchanging jokes, stories about wives or girlfriends. Some played cards or chess or watched the television in the dining hut. I was given a top bunk. It was in a corner, a position much prized because the two walls gave a measure of privacy which was denied those living in the centre. Below me was a young man with long hair, a deep broad chest, muscular arms and shoulders. His name was Raul. Raul was a typewriter mechanic in Havana. He was about thirty years old and had two small children. Altogether there were six brigades in the *campamento*, comprising a total of 200 men.

In the afternoon Pedrito, the brigade's leader, took me to the store and I was issued with a pair of boots, a straw sombrero, a glove for the left hand, a machete and a pair of black gauze goggles. The machete had a broad blade, slightly curved at the end. Raul eyed it with the glance of a professional, produced a file from a sheath in his belt and worked at the edge with long, even strokes. It was sharp as a razor when he handed it back. As darkness fell a full moon came up in front of the *campamento* and soon a dozen fires flared up over the cane fields. They would blaze for a few minutes like fireworks, sending up a column of smoke which could be seen clearly in the moonlight and then as suddenly die away. 'There's our work for tomorrow,' Raul said; 'all the cane that's burnt tonight must be cut tomorrow.'

This was the Australian method of cane cutting - to set the cane alight in carefully controlled squares so that the leaf was burnt away leaving only the cane stalk standing. Burnt cane, freed of the useless leaf, could be cut three times as fast. But the burnt cane must all be cut the next day - an extra day's standing would cause a drop in the sugar content. It was calculated so that the exact amount of cane was burnt that could be cut the next day.

At ten I went to bed in my top bunk. My brain was tumbling with half-digested thoughts and impressions. The hut seemed a grotesque place of stark shadows and outlines; the lattice frames of the bunks, the stars shining through an unglazed window, someone's clothes hanging from a hook in the ceiling, swinging gently in the draught like a suspended corpse. I felt an unreality as if my real self were somewhere else. I found it hard to understand how I could be where I was - what motives and urges had brought me into this place? What was I trying to achieve? What thing was inside me that I should be driven alone halfway across the world to find myself in this odd corner? I wasn't sure what I was seeking or whether I had found it. My thoughts were in disorder. Somewhere in the recesses of my mind *Iskra* was lying alongside the quay in Havana. My Dolphin was real, perhaps the only reality. I went to sleep when his droll form captured the foreground of my imagination.

I was woken at six. The lights were on, Pedrito was striding through the hut, 'Arriba brigada 37 - arriba - another day has come - another day of toil for the revolution - arriba.' Bodies were stirring, mosquito nets being thrust aside, black and brown and white legs were dangling from top bunks. There were muffled grunts and curses, someone started a sad song, someone else swore at it; there was the slow noise of men waking after sleep. I dashed handfuls of cold water in my face, put on trousers, a thick shirt, my new boots, my sombrero with the gauze goggles fastened round the brim by their elastic, grasped my machete. With Raul I made my way to the dining hut, stood in a subdued queue outside the hatch and was given a tin mug of thick milky coffee with a tin spoon in it. 'Keep the mug and spoon,' Raul said, 'they are yours

- don't lose them. You won't get another.' The coffee scalded and brought life. A lorry backed up to the dining hut and Pedrito herded his twenty *macheteros* up over the tailboard. 'Throw in your machete first,' Raul said; 'don't climb into the lorry with it in your hand - it's dangerous, you might hurt someone.' As the old lorry engaged first gear with a jerk and a grinding noise, the sun came up over the cane fields and suddenly it was day. The lorry jolted over rough tracks through the cane fields for two miles. Some of the *macheteros* stood against the uneven sway, grasping their sombreros against the wind, others sat on the floor of the truck. We arrived at the corner of a square of burnt cane. Machetes were thrown to the ground and the men jumped out.

We formed up in a line at the edge of the cane. Each man took four rows and the cutting began. Raul said, 'Don't try to go too fast. Cut the cane right down at the root with one stroke - soon you will be able to cut three or four stalks at one blow. Then lop off the tops and lay the cane neatly on your left so that the fork-lift

The machete rose and fell, my back began to ache

81

can pick it up. Work slowly and methodically - don't stop. Leave the roots cut back to the ground.'

At first I was clumsy and cut too high. 'That's where the sugar is, down at the bottom,' Raul said. 'You must cut low - leave the root clean so that the new plant can grow easily.' Soon I began to find a rhythm, to cut faster and to leave the ground clean. Even so, I fell behind and Raul would leave his own four rows and help me until I caught up. The fine black burnt dust flew in a thin cloud and clogged my nostrils, my ears, penetrated the gauze goggles, found its way under my clothes, into my boots. The sun rose in the sky and the sweat began to run, streaming down my face in white rivulets. The machete rose and fell, it seemed independently of any agency of mine. My back began to ache, my shoulders creaked, my right hand took the shape of the machete's handle. The sun climbed the sky and poured down its venom; there was no sound except the slicing machetes and the soft swish of the falling cane. Time seemed to fall apart - there was no end to this wilderness of cane, it went on forever, the men of Brigade 37 engulfed in cane. Their effort was meaningless against this infinity of dusty soldiers. However the Brigade advanced an inexhaustible reserve was always at attention in front of them, confident, like a Chinese army, in the power of numbers.

I looked behind the ragged line of *macheteros*. It seemed that we had moved no more than a few paces and already the sun was high above, sending its vertical rays without pity. I saw that I had fallen behind once again. Brigade 37 were not novices in the business of cutting cane. Pedrito, Raul and a dozen others had spent four *zafras* working through from March until July, with no break except two days in every thirteen. They were hard and thin. Their muscles were iron, their hands were leather plates. At ten the lorry came back along the track, leaving a puff of dust behind it. 'Merienda, merienda' - the word passed along the line.

Ignacio was a Spaniard, an older man than the others. I judged him to be in his fifties. He had got on the wrong side of the authorities in Spain and had been imprisoned in the Canary Islands for six years. Then he had escaped and made his way to Venezuela in an old trawler packed with immigrants. He was a man of intelligence and culture. He had come to Cuba and had prospered - was one of the managers of a group of radio and television technicians in Havana. He had been cutting cane ever since the first experiments in voluntary labour in 1964 and had only missed one *zafra* - the great *zafra* of the ten million tons in 1970. Ignacio had stayed behind that year, struggling to maintain an efficient repair service with his depleted work force. Everyone had gone to cut cane in 1970 and the result had been chaos.

The cane cutters were friendly and informal. If they didn't know what to make of the *Inglés* they were prepared to accept him as a compañero. Merienda lasted a brief quarter of an hour and then we were back at work. My right arm was a machine. My body began to fall into the rhythm of the work. Already I could cut three stalks at a time, straighten up, lop off the top leaves, turn and throw the cane down to my left and then move my feet into a new position, all in one movement. I noticed that the best *macheteros*, Raul among them, seemed to have perfected this rhythm, working unhurriedly but never stopping. Now the sun was brutal, the burnt cane offered no shade. I became aware of parts of my body for the first time, a muscle on the inside of my leg protested every time I moved my left foot, something seemed to be puncturing the small of my back, my belt was cutting into my side. Raul came over to help. 'The first three days are the worst. If you can stand after three days you'll make a *machetero*.' Time was measured by cane - the sun had stopped in its course, only the rhythm mattered.

At twelve I saw light through the jungle in front and soon the camp was finished. With a conscious effort I straightened my back and walked slowly across the stubble with Brigade 37, between the neat rows of stacked cane that would be lifted and taken to the *centrale* in the afternoon. Soon the lorry came and the Brigade climbed on board. I felt the refreshing breeze blow round me as the lorry rolled back through the cane to the *campamento* like a ship forging through a green ocean. The Brigade climbed out of the truck. I found my mug and my spoon on the floor under my bunk where I had left them, washed the emulsion of sweat and dust from my face and joined the queue in the dining hut. My mess tray was piled with rice, meat and thick brown soup, enough for six men.

The men ate their lunch in silence. Afterwards there was black coffee; then some played chess, some read and others went to sleep, stretched out full length on the ground in a corner of shade. My body had received a deep shock. This was work of a severity I had never experienced - I could not remember when I had worked with such intensity. Work might be monotonous and exacting, but no work in my experience was as hard as this. I understood for the first time the meaning of the word. This was not a job, it was work.

Pedrito came round again gathering up his brood and shepherding them out to the truck. This time we went further afield, past the campo we had cut in the morning to another on the other side of a low hill. Already as we passed the scene of our morning's work the forklift was loading the cane. This business of the *zafra* required a high degree of organisation; mustering volunteers, organising them into brigades, supplying them with provisions and clothing and tools at the *campamento* and planning the work so that the process could go ahead smoothly from day to day. There had been mistakes and confusion when the revolution first went into the business of cutting millions of tons of cane with voluntary labour - much waste of manpower, materials and time. Now things were better thought-out and more disciplined. At the beginning, enthusiasm had been wasted by bad organisation; now a carefully planned programme had taken the place of the euphoria of the early days.

Soon Brigade 37 were advancing step by step across another field of cane, soon the aches and strains of the morning were back. The afternoon sun was a fiercer enemy, the whole world was red hot; there was no escape, no indulgence. The Brigade worked steadily on, never slacking the pace. Raul would fall back and help me so that I straggled less obviously behind the line but now I was beginning to keep up better. Pedrito would come round from time to time and cast an eye on the work, never criticising but sometimes tidying some stump of cane that I had not cut to the base. At merienda in the afternoon I felt I had done better. At five the *campamento* was not quite finished and the Brigade worked on until nearly six so that burnt cane should not be left standing for the night. There was a feeling of satisfaction, a flood of pleasure and relief, a release of tension, as the men straightened their backs and looked over the field of stubble, the neat rows of felled cane. Already the fork lift was at work collecting it and loading it into trucks. There was banter and good humour as the Brigade straggled back across the campo to wait for the truck. I experienced a sensation of identity with these people; there was a flush of intimacy between us, a shared satisfaction in work well done. The sun went down, leaving behind a thousand million stars and the burning earth, left to cool for a spell.

The *campamento* was like home; my bunk as I had left it, my change of clothes in a pile under the mosquito net, a few books and a copy of *Bohemia*, my mug and spoon in my corner of the floor. These were the private, personal things in a communal life, things that belonged to me, things which filled an engrained need - possessions. I took my towel and the small piece of soap I had been given to the shower and scrubbed away at the cane dust. Already the *campamento* was coming to life - people were singing, exchanging jokes, bantering. 'How did the *Inglés* get on on his first day?' someone asked Raul. 'Fine, *carajo*, that boy can work. He will make a *machetero*.' I felt a tingle of pleasure.

The *macheteros* looked unfamiliar in their clean clothes as they made a loose queue with their mess trays for the evening meal. It was much like lunch except that it was fish instead of meat - the same great pile of rice and a thick soup. The food was monotonous but was dispensed in enormous quantities. After the meal Ignacio took me off in a jeep, with Pedrito and half a dozen others hanging to it like swarming insects. We drove through the cool night to tomorrow's camp. There was a discussion as to the direction and strength of the wind and the amount of cane that could be cut the next day and then the men spread out in a line along the windward side of the cane, gathering up small piles of dry leaf to be used as torches. At a word from Pedrito the torches were lit and set to the dry brittle undergrowth. In seconds there was a roar of flame and the campo was alight from end to end. Flames leapt into the night, the steady, destructive crackle of the blaze like machine gun fire. The heat came out of the campo in a wall, like heat from an open furnace door, and the night was filled with brief, livid energy. The men ran round the campo as the flames swept through to see that no spark jumped across the line of plough between the fields - eight campos were to be burnt that night, their location depending on the readiness of the cane for cutting. It was a spectacular show, soon over. In an hour it was done, the last spark had died and the cane soldiers stood gaunt and naked, the green and brown leaves turned to black dust; the stalks, soaked in juice, undamaged by the fire. It was late by the time we got back to the *campamento*. I was worn out. I shared a mug of coffee with Raul and Pedrito and Ignacio before bed.

'What makes you do it?' I asked. 'This work, this grind, year after year? Is there no end to cane?' 'Yes, there may be an end

Men ran round the campo as the flames swept through

to it,' Raul said, 'mechanisation. Before the revolution there were no machines at all. The *zafra* was worked by professional *macheteros*. They worked for four months and then starved for the rest of the year. Now there is full employment, the *macheteros* have got jobs, there's a shortage of labour. In a few years there will be machines to cut the cane, one machine doing the work of a hundred *macheteros*. Then there will be an end to it. We do it because we have to. Our country has to have the sugar so that we can buy machines to cut the cane.'

'You mean you have to cut cane?' I said, 'Isn't it voluntary?'

'Caray,' Ignacio said, 'you people don't understand. There are hundreds of volunteers. Everyone wants to cut cane; we have to select the best *macheteros*. We cut cane because we want to. It's our way of fighting - fighting against poverty. Yes,' he mused, 'in a few years the only people working in the *zafra* will be technicians, operating the machines that will release us from this work.'

'There's nothing wrong with work,' Pedrito said, 'better to have too much than none. Before, I was unemployed for three years. You can ask my señora what that was like - thrown out of work without hope, without dignity.'

'You've got to be educated to live without work,' Raul said. 'An uneducated man must have work or his soul dies of frustration. An educated man has resources; he needs leisure, knows how to use leisure. When all Cuba is educated we will be able to share work among the people and share the leisure. In your country people are afraid of unemployment because when they can't work their children suffer. In Cuba nobody goes hungry, nobody is afraid. There is still much to do before we can catch up with rich countries like yours,' he said, 'but when we do catch up we will be really rich because the people will be rich - rich in education, rich because the people will have rich minds and rich ideas.'

At ten the lights went out in the *campamento*. I climbed into my top bunk under the mosquito net, a wave of relaxation flushed the aches and the tiredness out of my body. In minutes I was sleeping like a child.

The next day the work seemed harder, the sun stronger, the dust more clinging. By mid-afternoon I thought I would never survive the day. On my third day I was able to keep up with Raul. Now the rhythm had got into me and I learnt how to be economical in my movements. Now I began to know the men in the brigade and to be on easy terms with them. The cane soldiers were still there in all their hordes, but I advanced on them with greater confidence. My right arm rose and fell with accuracy and resolve. As the sweat poured, I began to see myself as a soldier of the revolution, living through a blind war, struggling forward by the side of my comrades towards some shadowy glory. I was like a Puritan soldier, in the grip of hot emotion; I felt that right and justice were my allies. I began to understand that when the clichés were cut away, socialism had real meaning. No one would work at this pace and with this intensity except as a volunteer; no money could pay me enough to stretch my body and my spirit in this way. 'It's ideas that make people work,' Ignacio would say, 'money makes work into a mean thing. I've worked for a hundred bosses, but I've never worked as hard as this.'

'What about the bosses in the Party?' I asked. 'Do they work in this way?' 'Harder,' Ignacio said. 'We are the vanguard, we set the example - that's what being in the Party means. You don't get a soft job when you join the Party. You've got to give your life to the cause, fight and work for every hour of the day'.

87

'But aren't there any Party officials who've got soft jobs, who managed to get things for themselves, things for themselves that other people can't get, who live in luxury and don't work harder than they have to?' 'A few - there may be some who once they have 'el carnet en el bolsillo' - their Party card in their pocket - sit back and take it easy but they soon get weeded out. There is criticism within the Party - criticism of people's private lives as well. I don't say that everyone in the Party is an angel, certainly not; but you can soon get thrown out. The Party has to maintain standards, Party members have to live with discretion. There are plenty of people down below who want to come up and who are prepared to make sacrifices. People with positions of power are vulnerable - why, look at the way Fidel himself lives! He isn't surrounded by luxury, he doesn't live in a palace. He works as hard as anyone in Cuba and he lives a simple life. Surely you understand that it would be impossible to persuade the people in this *campamento* to work at this pace voluntarily if they did not know in their hearts that they are working for all the people? If these people believed that they were working to keep a class of bureaucrats in soft jobs - why, the whole system would collapse.'

'It's hard to get into the Party,' Raul broke in, 'you have to be an exemplary worker, you have to have a high moral standard, you have to study.'

Pedrito said, 'We make sure that the Party does not become an elite, divorced from the hopes and needs of the people, but rather a group who can take responsibility, take decisions. There must be discipline. Without discipline and a sense of purpose we would be weak and in our position, so isolated from our friends, if we were weak the revolution would fail.'

As the work went on from day to day I became as resistant as any member of the Brigade. I found I was as good a worker as some although I could never match Raul's concentrated pace. The *macheteros* were the cream of workers. They were paid the same salary as in their normal jobs, they received a holiday when the harvest was over. Raul and Pedrito would go with their families to one of the beach resorts - places of luxury in the old days, places like Veradero which I had visited in *Iskra*. They would wear a badge to show that they had worked through the sugar harvest and this would entitle them to priorities; cinema seats, restaurant bookings, night clubs. They would go back to their work in Havana, taking with them a sense of virtue and self-satisfaction. Pedrito said, 'Voluntary work is the only kind of work worth doing. If you know you don't have to do it the work itself creates its own reward.'

I found that I was sharing a sense of purpose in this gruelling work. I would face the cane soldiers for hours on end, striking them down and advancing step by step and side by side with these people of Brigade 37 who had become my companions. My mind would fall into a trance-like oblivion. I would end each day covered in sweat and cane dust, consumed by the blazing sun, tired in body, bent and aching. I would wash under the cool shower in the evening, exchanging jokes with the Brigade as if I had lived among them all my life, conserving my single bar of soap with the economy of necessity. In the evening I would drink hot sweet strong coffee out of my tin mug, play chess or watch the trivialities of the television, or talk with Ignacio or Raul or Pedrito. Cubans are great debaters - about socialism and sugar and women they would talk all night.

On my last day in the *campamento* the Brigade stopped work an hour early. There was excitement, like school on the last day of term. I packed my belongings into my kit bag, handed in my mug and tin spoon, and the Brigade climbed into a lorry and set off for Havana. The sun foundered in a sea of cane, Martinez Prieto melted into the hot evening air. As the lorry came over the rise behind the *campamento* the fires were already burning; black fingers of smoke drifted lazily down wind, the walls of the *campamento* blazing pink in the oblique light - walls that I would never forget.

VIII

Storm

I met Lourdes again; the year after Iskra left Havana I went back in an aeroplane to see her. It was both a honeymoon and a swansong, an attempt to settle tangled emotions. I could never go to live in Cuba. As the old man had told me in Baracoa, 'There's no liberty'. Like solitude, liberty is a drug, if you've once had it you can't live without it. Most Cubans have never had it, consequently they don't miss it. They believe, genuinely, that the system they live under is one of liberty. In some respects it is. Lourdes was prepared to trade liberty for honest clean government, for the new sense of purpose the revolution had brought, for the sake of her children and because she loved her country. There were aspects of the revolution she feared and mistrusted - the ever-increasing power of the bureaucracy, the military adventures, the increasing discipline. Things were changing quickly.

I arrived at Havana airport uninvited by the government, a few days before the Cubans imposed visa restrictions against the British. Relations between Britain and Cuba had been good but they deteriorated rapidly during the 1970s. There was a sudden clamp-down. The Britain-Cuba friendship association was closed down, to the dismay of people who had worked for it for years. A friend of mine was subjected to horrifying interrogations when he was caught hitch-hiking in Oriente province. My easy friendship with people at the Embassy was at an end. I had come on a private visit, loaded with gifts for many friends, including a substantial box of toys for one of the *circulos* - day nurseries - in Havana. Everything was confiscated at the airport and it took all Lourdes' formidable force of character and charm to get any of it back. We spent a month together, we were watched by a kind of 'agent provocateur' who insinuated himself into our lives, drove us about in a motor car he happened to have, with petrol he happened to be able to get. He was so transparent that we were able to take advantage of his astonishing ability to get whatever we needed, without ever saying anything that could be construed as anti-revolutionary in answer to his leading questions. Neither of us was anti-revolutionary. He drove us to the Isle of Youth, which

I had been to in *Girl Stella* but which Lourdes had never seen. He procured us tickets for the ballet, the best outside Russia some say.

Lourdes and I went on a bus to Varadero and stayed in a beach hut which was owned by one of her uncles; we took part in that most astonishing annual exercise in political euphoria, Cuba's national day on July 26th, when a million people gather in Havana's 'Plaza de la Revolución' to be harangued by Fidel Castro for upwards of two hours. I found it difficult to live in Cuba without being a part of the official machine, an invited guest, a member of a delegation, a tourist on an organised holiday. No provision was made for an ordinary visitor, no ration book, no way to get a meal in a hotel, buy a pair of socks or a tube of toothpaste. When I left I too was subjected to an interrogation which lasted for two days. I was released just in time to catch the plane back to England. Five years later I tried to get a visa to visit Cuba again and to write articles for *The Guardian* newspaper. I submitted my application together with a supporting letter from the newspaper. Bolaños, my old friend, was now the ambassador in London but the visa never came. The Cubans never forgave me for falling in love in their country. The last I saw of Lourdes was on the balcony of Havana airport. As she waved, the tears welled out of her big, brown eyes and ran in a flood down her dark cheeks.

Iskra left Havana, homeward bound, on April 1st 1971, as I had told the Cubans she would when I arrived in Baracoa. I believe they were tired of me by the time I left, which was not surprising. There was a hint of relief at my departure - as if I were an old aunt who had outstayed her welcome. The officials were courteous and correct in every way until my last day, but the warmth had gone. I never paid for Iskra to be slipped and her bottom painted in the yard in Havana. Arturo gave me a letter on my last day which read, 'The charges incurred for Iskra's stay in the yard, hauling out on the slip, minor repairs and boat work have been paid for voluntarily by the workers'. As I sailed out into the Florida Strait they stood along the quay and waved. People came in a steady stream to wish me goodbye. I was showered with gifts. My flirtation with Cuba was over, never to be resurrected. I believe my Dolphin was happy to get away, to be at sea again in the clean purgative ocean, away from the deceits and compromises of the shore. It had been a near thing, he thought. For a time it had looked as if he would never get away, would have to learn to be a Communist Dolphin and swim only with the stream, constricting his wayward wanderings to a path set by some aloof, all-powerful master Dolphin who would know best for him, would guide him, even force him, to swim in one direction. As Iskra began to dip into the turbulence of the Florida Strait the waves washed him clean - a symbolic ablution.

The fine weather that I had been given by the Havana Institute of Oceanography, illustrated with coloured wind charts and bound in parchment, left me within half an hour. It began to blow hard from the north-east, against the four-knot current that sweeps through the Florida Strait to form the Gulf Stream. Rough seas came tumbling aboard. Iskra began to force herself forward against them, hitting them squarely with a brave but ineffective display of aggressiveness, sometimes burying her bows in green water. I double-reefed the mainsail, reefed the staysail and changed to a smaller jib, becoming wet and cross. Below, the violent motion unseated a dozen kindly meant keepsakes that had

been pressed into my hands, competing with one another to create chaos in the cabin. A wooden ash tray manoeuvred itself into position to batter a glass ornament which shattered, spreading tiny crystals across the cabin. A box of cigars sprung open and embraced freedom with joy, rolling in and out of a narrow strip of water which had already found its way to the lee side, so that they became molten cylinders, oozing a brown juice. A bottle of rum was spilt across the mat, giving off an unwholesome vapour. A parcel of ornamental men spewed out a small brigade who rolled back and forth across the broken glass like drunken fakirs. In another hour the wind freshened again and the double-reefed mainsail was too much for her.

By the time I had taken it in and set the storm trysail in its place I was tired, wet, shivering, miserable. It was already dark. Behind, the glow of Havana flushed across the black sky, ahead and to port I could see the lights of Key West. The sudden transition to solitude was harder to bear this time perhaps. I had been so much a part of everything just a few hours ago and now I was quite alone, surrounded by an empty, inhospitable sea intent on making life hard. My friends of the morning were still there, going about their affairs; I was in another world. There was no link between me and yesterday save an odd thought, perhaps a casual concern for my welfare. Lourdes would worry for a bit but soon that wound would heal too.

I was undecided where I should go. I could hardly put in to Miami even if I had any wish to. It was a hotbed of anti-Castro Cuban exiles; I would be lucky to come out of the place alive. Freeport, to starboard, was a possible haven for me. I would be able to get all the stores I wanted there, rest and coax myself into a better mental state for the 1,200-mile passage to Bermuda and then the Atlantic crossing. The Gulf Stream would take me close to the place - I could be there the next day. I dithered as Iskra forged through the strait, with the current taking her in every direction like a twig borne by a swift river. I nearly wrecked her on the Florida Keys, waking in the night to see that she had been swept in-shore by the Stream so that I could see a lighthouse to seaward. I put about in panic, already in the shallows, with the low, indistinct outline of the mangrove islands close aboard and clawed offshore, a river of cold sweat running down my back, my body shaking with fear. If I went into Freeport there would be explaining to be done. What had I been doing in Cuba? Why was

I alone? It was illegal to enter the Bahamas from Cuba. On the other hand I had only a few biscuits left and my bread was already gone; my tins had been depleted, I had given most of them to Lourdes and to friends. Everything had been difficult to get in Cuba, even at the diplomatic shop. I was short of fresh food, had no potatoes and I wanted to repair Iskra's electric pump.

I had become used to making decisions at once and sticking to them. This time I veered from side to side like a neurotic. The weather came fine after I had been out for a day and a night, when Freeport was under my lee, but I still couldn't make up my mind. Then, when I might still have gone there, the wind swung to the south putting Freeport to windward, the bottom dropped out of the barometer, a huge black cloud spread over the sky, clamping itself over my world like an iron lid, the wind began to freshen. If a man won't make his mind up at sea the ocean will do it for him. Iskra cleared the Mantilla Shoal at the extreme north of the Bahamas Chain and set course into the wide ocean, out into the gathering storm as the night set in.

A gale at sea for a man alone is a subjective experience, in retrospect he can never be certain how fierce the wind was, how destructive the waves, even that it was a gale. Iskra has no instruments on board with which to gauge the strength of the wind. I base my assessment of a gale on the memory I have carried with me for most of my life of a gale I experienced, in a ship, in the Southern Ocean off Cape Horn. To me, that gale is the yardstick I offer up to it all other gales for comparison. It was during the war, I was in my early 'teens, one of the apprentices in an old, rusty steamer called the *Celtic Star*, homeward bound to Liverpool from Buenos Aires. Because of German surface raiders in the Atlantic the ship was routed home round Cape Horn to Valparaiso, then through the Panama Canal to Cuba, Halifax Nova Scotia and across the Atlantic. I was on the wheel, steering the ship down the River Plate, when the Captain opened his secret instructions and I saw the look of astonishment spread over his countenance. When we came out of the river we turned south.

It was August - winter time in the Southern Ocean. As we sighted Cape Horn the gale hit us. The seas grew to such a size that the ship was made small by them, as if she had been reduced by some weird alchemy. Each journey from one crest to the next was a voyage in itself, through a grey wilderness of smaller waves within the compress of the huge swell, each small wave enough to shake the ship as it swept over the bows, submerging the whole of the fore-part with a wild surge of broken water. When she came to the top of each swell, with its toothed battlement of breaking waves, the ship would groan and shudder and bend as the sea passed under her, the propeller racing, half out of the sea, shaking her whole being, the old iron hull warping as if on a wheel of torture. When she rolled she went over as if she would never come back, poised on her beam ends, undecided whether to roll on to infinity and the bottom; then slowly, reluctantly, recovering her stability. The boats were torn from the davits, ventilator cowls, iron stanchions, the bridge ladder, were bent like child's toys, hurled to the ground in a fit of rage. I remember watching her from the bridge, wondering in a detached way, as if I had no part in her travail, whether she would come through; wondering how I would fare in this ocean if I was ever to find myself in it on board a yacht. My experience of the sea is set against the backcloth of that gale. I have feared it and at the same time been fascinated by it and drawn towards it. I have always known that, one day, I would have to face it. I sometimes believe that the purpose of my wanderings in small boats has been to bring on this confrontation.

The wind freshened quickly and the sea began to build up on Iskra's quarter, taking on the surly, threatening aspect that is a certain precursor of a gale. It had a leaden, opaque look, a special malevolence, a prescription for violence. I prepared Iskra for what was to come; changed to the storm trysail, took down the mainsail and lashed it to the boom gallows, took in the jib, set a small staysail, doubled the sheet, checked lashings, pumped the bilge, filled a vacuum flask with hot soup. Then I wrote up my journal because I know that writing soothes me, eases the fear. There is a permanence, a feeling of reliability about the written word, a suggestion that what has been started will remain to be finished. This was not the sudden, anguished fear that had flushed through me when Iskra had come near to grounding on the Keys, but a deeper, more profound disquiet that stirred round my inside making it hollow with apprehension. I had put myself into danger by my own vacillations - Iskra could have been in Freeport harbour if I had read the weather correctly and had acted decisively. Instead she was out in the most dangerous sector of the Bermuda triangle in a rising gale and ill-prepared to face it.

I was in no fit state to withstand bad weather - I was tired and had not yet fallen into my sea routine of sleep. The journey through the Florida strait had been unnerving and unsettling, I was short of stores, the electric pump hadn't been repaired. When my mind cast itself forward into the empty spaces of ocean between Iskra and Bermuda I was afraid. I wrote, 'We're going to be punished tonight - black clouds are racing across the sky high up and below them squalls of cold rain. Thank God I've got some room now - we're clear of that bloody strait. I can just see the loom of Miami right astern. It's a thousand miles to Bermuda - Christ. Those stories of the triangle, I wonder if there's anything in them? I hope the poor old boat stays in one piece. I must go to sleep before it all blows up.' I looked round the dark seascape. The grey ocean merged into a grey sky, so that the line between was a blurred, hazy emulsion that seemed to be closing in on Iskra with the last of the light. She was the only real thing in a world of threat and unknown imaginings. I put in the hatch board, lay down on the lee bunk with a heavy blanket pulled over me and slept deeply. My Dolphin smiled in his wisdom.

I woke four hours later with the crash of green water on the deck. I looked at the clock, 'Christ, how could I have been asleep for so long?' As I slid open the hatch and looked out another sea broke aboard, flooding the cockpit, spilling over the deck, pouring through the open hatch like an extrusion of some solid substance, soaking the chart table and the bunk. Bilge water was slopping across the cabin sole. I cursed, put on my harness, watched for a moment and then climbed out into the cockpit. The wind had freshened to a gale. Iskra had luffed, putting the seas forward of the beam so that they broke aboard. Through the blackness of the night I could see them advancing on her like soldiers in line of battle, each wave with a white plume, breaking into roundshot and flung by the wind down its front and into the face of the next in line, peppering it with white wounds. She was on her side, racing through it like some frightened animal, her tiny sails pinning her down so that the seas swept over her unimpeded, or struck square against her starboard side sending heavy water in a solid mass into her square of trysail. The wind's voice had an edge of insanity grafted to its muted, full-throated roar.

I slipped the chain off the tiller and swung the helm over. Iskra hesitated and then began to turn. As her stern was forced round another sea hit her quarter. For an instant I was submerged in green water tumbling all over me from somewhere above, pulling, wrenching at me as I clung to the tiller, blinding me so that I could see only the dim, green outline of the hatch and the fore part of the cockpit. I thought she was sinking - that I was going down and down into the centre of this green world. She seemed to shudder and shake herself. She came upright and the sea poured off her, cascading out through the scuppers, down through the cockpit floor into the bilge, off the cabin top to fill the side decks with bubbling, fizzing champagne. I slid open the hatch and looked below. The water was halfway up the floor - the chart, the kettle, my cane-cutting sombrero were floating serenely, slopping from side to side with Iskra's uneven roll. How had I slept for so long? Where was my mechanism that tells me of danger? She must have luffed and brought the seas on the beam in the last few minutes, her storm trysail, with the freshening gale in it, overpowering the vane steering.

I settled her on course - at least the wind was fair, she was pointing in the right direction but she was going too fast. She was racing the seas instead of going with them. She would surf on top of a wave and then slide down its front so that the next would catch her in the trough and wash over her. I clipped my harness to the lifeline, went for'ard moving from hold to hold, watching where I would put my hands, where I would fix my foot before I let go of one secure position for another. The foredeck was a tiny triangle, leaping and twisting its way through the ocean. Sometimes the bow wave would plume up on either side of the stem, the wind would snatch it away and scatter it into a million particles. Poor Dolphin - he would be wishing he was back in the fleshpots of Havana.

When she surfed she would ride the wave like a circus acrobat, turning herself from side to side as she was borne along on a bubbling cushion of surf, hissing and spitting foam, out of the control of her steering gear. I reached for the pin-rail at the foot of the mast and let go the trysail halyard, easing it gently down and gathering in the heavy folds of cloth, taking one of the tyers from round my neck and securing the sail to the boom. That trysail is a friend - it slides down the mast like a gentleman. She was eased at once, I moved my position to the cabin top, securing the trysail with two more tyers. Now she was steady and within herself.

I looked around. My world seemed to have contracted itself to the narrow circle of my vision. The white crests were like neon lights winking on and off in some strange wonderland, diminishing as they faded into the black perimeter that ringed me round. Iskra too had a kind of luminosity, given her by a faint diffusion of the moon, which had secreted itself high above the dense layers of cloud. I could see the steering vane standing erect and rigid in the wind, guiding her through the seas; the sheets, the runners, bar tight with strain, holding her in restraint; the tiller moving with logical, incisive thrust in response to the shift of course and wind and sea. She looked tight and strong. She was in control again. She gave off a confidence which communicated itself to me so that I was no longer afraid.

I went back to the cockpit, looked around again and reached for the pump. I could sit on the bridge deck and work the pump with one hand, glancing below as the level went slowly down, glancing at the compass, at the seas and marvelling at Iskra's cleverness, her dexterity, as she swerved and dodged through them. Now, without the trysail, she was slower and safer. The waves passed under her, moving steadily ahead of her so that she slotted herself into the spaces behind them, keeping her way, ready and in command of herself before the next one came up with her. She seemed easiest with the wind and the seas slightly on one of her quarters. The staysail was sheeted in tight; it must be kept full of wind. If the wind came astern and shook it, the sheet cringle would be torn out and the sail would be shredded. Soon the cabin was dry; the chart, my sombrero, the kettle still with its spout cocked up in defiance, were grounded on the cabin sole. I climbed below into the warmth and safety of her.

The flask was still jammed in its place behind the galley where I had left it - my cold, wet, stiff joints rejoiced in the still, warm air. When I slid the hatch closed it was suddenly quiet, as if I had passed from a city street through the revolving doors of some plush emporium. This was home, safety, comfort from the storm. I found a pair of trousers, a shirt, a sweater that was dry. I poured a cup of steaming soup, wedged myself on the port bunk beside the chart table, allowed the hot strengthening liquid to flood into the empty spaces of my stomach, bringing comfort, warmth, confidence. The lamp swung in its gimbol, throwing its moving shadows against the varnished cabin sides, filling my world with a soft light. I retrieved the chart, wiped it dry and placed it on the chart table again, restored the kettle to its place on the galley stove, tapped the barometer. It was low but it jumped upwards.

The motion inside was violent but steady. With no more than a handkerchief of staysail she was running through the storm on an even keel, rolling, heavily at times, first one way and then the other, but always recovering herself. 'If this is the worst it can do', I said aloud, 'we've beaten it.' My Dolphin smiled in his wisdom. It is a common fault to believe the war is already won after the first battle. I tapped the glass again before I went to sleep. It jumped up again. Something in the back of my mind whispered to me, 'quick rise after low, foretells a stronger blow', but I shrugged my shoulders and lay down on the lee bunk under my blanket.

I went to sleep thinking of Lourdes, wondering what sort of havoc I had created in her life and she in mine, wondering how it could ever be resolved, wondering at the shifts of emotion, the wayward chance that brings people together and thrusts them apart again. Dolores, thousands of miles away in La Palma had brought us together; the wreck of the *Girl Stella*, as many thousands of miles ahead of me in Flores, had wrenched Celia and me apart. Celia had lost her confidence in me, perhaps in herself as well, when *Girl Stella*'s two masts sank below the waves of Puerto Piqueran. She had told me this at the time - I believe she had been as much attached to *Girl Stella* as I to Iskra and the culpable loss of her had made a wound which would never heal. Celia had no liking for Iskra and would have no truck with her. Perhaps Iskra herself, the Dolphin, was my real love? Certainly at this moment I had better love him - only he stood between me and destruction.

Was I in love with the sea, finding in the ocean a response to my feelings and moods which no person could provide? There is justice in the ocean, a discipline which I am in sympathy with; its retribution is terrible, it is impartial, omnipotent, containing a life within its hand to preserve or destroy as its whim dictates. It rewards virtue, or good fortune, with beauty, which is the ultimate gift. It is not transitory, its embrace is forever. My Dolphin, which is part of Iskra and at the same time part of the ocean, was more real, more reliable, more lasting. If he could not love, at least he could mirror my joys, sorrows, aspirations.

I woke in an hour, immediately aware of Iskra's motion - the sound of the wind, her more sudden, stiff movement containing a new threat. She had altered course a point to the north - the wind must have backed. I got up at once. The barometer had gone down to a new low, wiping out its brief rise. I put on my wet gear, safety harness, climbed out of the cabin, stepping over the wash board, sliding the hatch closed behind me. It was blowing harder. The dawn was already paling the horizon, the seas were bigger, the cloud was closer, darker, the whine of the wind was shrill in the rigging. I looked for'ard at the staysail. The sheets were rigid with strain, the luff of the sail stretched against the forestay, climbing aloft in eliptical steps from hank to hank, the naked bowsprit buried itself and shook itself free as every wave passed under her. The brown sail made a small patch of dark against grey cloud, swaying across the sky with the boat's roll.

Then my eye picked out a triangle of light above the clew of the sail. I could see it, even from the cockpit. That was a tear - I could see it. I climbed for'ard up the lee deck and looked closely at the sail. The stitches were gone along the bottom cloth. The strain was already forcing the cloths apart; the wind was already nagging and worrying at this small breach, quick to exploit a weakness. Soon the stitches would run, the sail would shake, the wind would get behind it and tear it apart. Without her staysail Iskra would broach; with no sail to keep her head before the seas she would fall broadside to them and be overwhelmed. I looked from side to side at the troughs and the breaking seas behind and knew that her only safety lay in keeping her stern to the seas. I had no other staysail, only the storm jib. It would be difficult, perhaps impossible to set it: to bend on the sheet, to fix its tack to the bowsprit traveller, to hoist it, flapping and shaking like a demented creature - it would pull the mast out of her. She was safe for as long as the strain of the wind was steady and even - once it took charge, once a sail got loose, something was certain to break. I climbed back to the cockpit. It could only be minutes before it tore - perhaps half an hour with luck. Could I repair it without taking the sail down? I might. It was worth a try.

I climbed below again, went for'ard. Under the bench in the fo'c'sle was the bo'suns's box, in it my smart sailmaker's roll, 'Ratsey & Laphorn' stencilled on the outside. I'd be too mean to buy anything like that now, I thought to myself. I took a small needle, threaded a yard of twine, pulled it through a block of beeswax, fixed the needle to the front of my jacket, slipped the palm into my pocket and climbed back to the foredeck. It was light now, the day had arrived stealthily, as if reluctant to displace the night, throwing a dreary light over this madness of sea. By sitting on the foredeck, my back pressed against Iskra's cabin side, the safety harness clipped round the mast, I could reach the sail. The split had run another four inches, already the edges of the cloth were beginning to flap and the sail was being forced out of shape by the wind. I was just in time. I put the needle through the end hole left by the old stitch, pulled it to the knot and drew the thread through; then I pushed it through the other way and then back again. I made half a dozen stitches and then gently pulled each one tight. It was like sewing a balloon - each time I pulled the stitches through I thought the material would tear, but it held. I stitched to the end of the tear and beyond for extra strength and then worked back, using the holes of the opposite zigzag to make the seam good. Each time Iskra shipped a sea it came curling round the cabin side and soaked me, sometimes lifting me against my braced feet and against the pull of the harness. I knotted the end and cut the twine, pleased with my work. The sail was old; it looked strong but when it was taut with strain I could see each single stitch fulfilling the hope and promise of its making.

I made my way back to the cockpit. This was going to be a long fight. This was the survival storm I had read about in books, had talked about in yacht club bars, had lived with in my imagination all my life. This was the test, the only valid test, myself against my own weakness - weakness of physical might, of endurance, of intelligence, of the will to come through. Lourdes, Celia, my children, the whole fetch of my life, held no relevance here. There were only two moments in my existence, one backwards in time to that day in the Southern Ocean when the old tramp steamer battled for her life, the other now, in this other ocean, in the old tramp Iskra with my Dolphin tucked under her bow, battling for our lives too.

The wind was stronger again. When Iskra was on top the force of it tore at my clothes, forced me down into the cockpit, an invisible weight pressing from above. The vane steered her faultlessly as if it were graced with understanding, able to predict the set of the seas and make adjustments as it saw fit. Each time she rose to a sea it seemed to assess her needs, tilt itself one way or the other, or remain rigid and erect to pilot her down into the hollow, repeating its deft and skilful adjustments tirelessly and without fault. If the wind freshened again I would stream a warp over the stern to slow her down.

I wondered what my friends and the people I loved would make of this, if they could imagine it. It was outside their understanding - they would find it impossible to envisage this extremity of experience. I was not certain I knew why I was in this position. I re-thought the old reasoning I had used before to bolster my confidence. It was by my own choice - no one was paying me to do it, I was in search of no honour. I knew that there was something inside me, some small, festering itch that had been wrapped up all my life. There was a desire to test myself, gauge the limits of my capacity, discover a serenity that had always eluded me - the reaction to an inborn unrest, a bizarre urge that demanded expression. At all events the Atlantic would blow these conceits out of my system. If it was a confrontation with nature that I had been seeking, I was face to face with it now.

I watched her all day, anxiously examining her gear, keeping the bilge dry, on the look-out for chafe to the vane lines or to the staysail sheets. She was within herself. If it didn't get worse she would come through. I was getting tired but I was confident, even triumphant - I was proud of my boat. This gale was not as fierce

as the Southern Ocean had been all those years ago but it was of
the same order, in the same class. My mind went forward to when
it would be over, to the quiet joy of nostalgia when I could look
back on it.

In the early evening the staysail blew out. I had been half
expecting it. My stitching had given a few hours' grace at least
and I had worked out in my mind what I could do when it
happened. I heard it and felt it from the cabin. Iskra shuddered
as if she had struck a solid object. There was a slatting and a
thundering like a train in a sudden tunnel. When I looked
through the hatch the sail had gone, dissolved into the wind,
nothing left but a few ragged tails of material clinging to the luff
rope which still straggled up the fore stay. Iskra lost way; the tight,
controlled triangle of force between her staysail which had given
her power, her grip on the water through her length and the
careful conning of the vane, was at once upset. She became
sluggish and unmanageable. Now her stern would swing away
from the wind and the vane's full scope was hardly enough to
bring her before it again. I had the storm jib ready to set in place
of the staysail, tied in a tight bundle and folded so that its head

and its foot were ready to hand when I came to bend it on. I checked that I had everything with me - shackle key, knife, a spare fastening to the sheet - clipped on my harness and climbed for'ard, the sail under my arm. I had rehearsed in my mind how I was to do it.

I jammed the bundle of sail in the space between the mast and the fore part of the cabin where it would stay firmly wedged until I needed it. I undid the staysail halyard, worked my way for'ard until I was in the very bows of the ship, clipped my harness to the forestay and began to haul down the luff of the torn sail so that I could recover the top of the halyard. The wind wrapped me round, pressing my jacket and trousers to the contours of my body. I clung to the stay as if it were the last piece of matter left on earth. The hanks of the old sail, still fastened to the stay, had turned themselves round and round it, jamming the halyard halfway up the stay so that I had to untwist it before I could get it down. It came foot by foot and then it would come no further. I tried to free it by pulling first on the halyard and then down on the ragged remains of the luff but something was holding it. I looked up and saw that one of the hanks had turned over itself, jamming itself against the stay. It was just out of my reach. I stretched up my full reach - couldn't quite grasp the last hank. The wind was trying to stream me off to lee'ard like a flag. I stood up on Iskra's anchor bits to give myself another foot and a half of height, reached above my head, grasped the top hank and began to untwist. The tiny triangle of deck at Iskra's bow, with the wild ocean all round, was the loneliest place on earth. Then she broached-to.

I didn't see the wave coming because it was behind me. I felt her lift and slew round, the mast tilted to starboard, I turned my head and saw the sea leaping at me, a huge thing towering up above, all unsteady, the top already curling over on itself, taken by the wind and shredded to a white mist. Iskra's stern seemed to be pivoting round, flying through the air. Then it was on me and I was carried away, suddenly weightless and free, turning slowly over and round within a cocoon of water, faintly luminous, green, surprisingly warm, soft like cotton wool. It occurred to me that this was the end. I came up with a jerk that shook the breath out of me. I was in the sea by Iskra's bow, next to my Dolphin, and on the same level, so that for an instant we were beside each other in the sea. I saw his face, grinning at me as if the whole affair was a huge joke. Iskra's rail was level with my head, her foredeck sloping upwards. I grabbed at the anchor lashed to the deck, swung my leg and my hip over the rail and as she slowly righted herself she dragged me out of the sea and left me like a piece of seaweed lying on the deck. I got up, unclipped my harness from the forestay and worked my way aft, clipping it again to the lifeline.

Now the seas were on her port beam, she wallowed in the trough at their mercy. The next crest broke over her as I got to the cockpit, washing over her and tumbling down the still-open hatch. I slammed the hatch shut, cursing myself for a careless idiot, disconnected the steering vane and swung the tiller over to port - she had lost her way. She would never answer her helm, the tiller was limp in my hand, kicking and jerking ineffectively like a dying animal. I ran for'ard again. The foredeck had been swept clean - the storm jib had gone from behind the mast. I had no means of turning her before the wind again.

I remember my mind racing as I stood in the cockpit and watched the seas batter my boat. They would crash down over the whole length of her, hitting at her with mindless violence. It would only be time before they broached her meagre defence. Her cabin top was of teak, fashioned all those years ago by craftsmen who meant it to last, her frames of English oak, her gear as good as could be provided. Of what consequence was this excellence against a force of overwhelming strength, hammering at the gates of her safety? I had no sail I could use to take her head to lee'ard, even if I could recover the halyard. Her span was to be measured in minutes now. The staysail was gone, the storm jib was gone, the working jib was below but I knew I could never set it, the reaching staysail was a voluminous garment of light nylon, irrelevant to these conditions. I could see no swift improvisation that would save her.

I went below - perhaps if I looked over my resources I might see some way out. All was confusion below. Water was over the cabin floor again, surging over the lee bunk every time a wave hit her and she lurched away from it. The noise of the hammering seas was suddenly sinister. I could almost feel the coach roof give each time a load of green water fell on it. The kettle had got loose again, the cover of the engine had been wrenched off and was adrift. As I slammed it back in position I glanced at the engine, all green painted, its flywheel half under water. 'Christ - the engine; perhaps the bloody engine would start? It must be full of water, but it might - it's worth a try.' I found the crank, flung over the decompression lever and began to turn. I swung it until the fly wheel was turning fast and then I pushed the electric starter and it engaged with a growl. I let go the crank and released the decompression lever - it fired with a great bang. A column of water fountained out of the engine well, scooped up by the fly wheel. She was already in gear. She began to move forward. I jumped through the hatch, swung the tiller, saw her bow pay off, her stern swing against those advancing white crests. Then the engine stopped.

I knew it must stop but it didn't matter. Once she was before the wind I could keep her on course by steering her myself. The vane couldn't give her enough helm to keep her before the wind unless she was moving at two or three knots - without sail her speed wasn't more than one knot and she needed the full swing of her rudder to keep her at it. I knew the fuel tanks would have water in them. They were under the deck in the stern where they had been half submerged in water for a day. It must have forced itself in, through the filler caps perhaps or through the air inlet. The filter was near the tanks but the run of pipe between the filter and the engine would have been full of clean oil. As soon as this was used and water got through to the injectors the engine had to stop. But it had saved her.

It took me an hour to pump her dry, standing with the tiller between my legs, leaning forward and working the pump with my right hand. In the last of the light I saw the water go down below the cabin floor, leaving its flotsam of gear behind. The kettle was on its side, rolling across the floor and battering itself against the bunk sides, without its spout. I couldn't leave the tiller to go to its rescue. I was chained to the tiller now. I was cold, hungry, tired - frightened now that the immediate danger was over. It had never occurred to me to be frightened but now, as the sequence of events billowed and swirled across my mind, I shuddered. The gale wasn't over, the barometer was still falling, the sky was the same low, menacing cover, the seas were rougher now - I had never seen anything like this from the deck of a yacht. I began to wonder whether I could come through it, how long it would go on for. Could this wind blow for ever, piling up the seas one over the other, one behind the other, until the whole scene took on an aspect of mad, destructive confusion?

With the night, the wind freshened and the seas became steeper and less true in direction. Iskra was shipping heavy water.

I was chained to the tiller now, I was cold, hungry, tired

Sometimes a rogue wave running at an angle to the general on-rush would climb her quarter and fall with studied violence on the after part of the boat. Sometimes she would avoid them, cleverly side-stepping and slewing her stern so that they thundered harmlessly alongside. Sometimes she would be caught and the water would fill the cockpit and flood the deck. With the moon the wind rose to a shrill steady scream driving out all other sound. The waves abandoned their uniformity. They seemed to move in on Iskra, assailing her from all sides so that she fumbled and was confused. With her stern pointing in line with the seas she was safe, offering the least resistance she took the least punishment. As long as she ran at the right speed and in the right direction she could be kept from danger.

In seas of such a size and of such power I could not leave the vane to steer. It could not see, it could only feel the wind. I sat on the bridge deck facing aft, with the safety harness clipped to one of the lifelines, and studied the topography of the seas. I found that I could steer with one hand on the tiller, the other working the pump. My clothes were wet, I was cold, but the concentration, the narrowing of my mind to this single effort, did not allow awareness of discomfort. I could survive only by using every aspect of my intelligence. If I could keep it up for long enough Iskra would come through. If I left the tiller she would take heavy water on board; at worst she would broach-to again and if she broached now she would sink. Exposed to the fury of these seas along her full length, I knew that she could not survive. I had heard a dozen discussions, had read the books - to heave-to in a storm, to run before it, to lie a-try, leaving the boat to her own devices, to find her own comfort. Now the reality of it left no doubts. If I allowed Iskra to fall broadside to the oncoming waves she would be overwhelmed.

I had no wish to drown but I was not afraid of drowning. If I had to die it was a natural death. I had often wondered how it would be. I imagined a great peace, that I would be able to face drowning without rancour or remorse. I had played with the sea, taken chances with it, tried its patience and flirted with its moods - I could not complain if at last the sea tired of the game. I could imagine the water clutching and dragging at my body. At first I would struggle to stay afloat, fight a meaningless action to prolong life in the inconceivable hope of rescue. Then I would come to understand that this was the end, the final episode. I would feel the salt in my mouth, hear the roar of the sea in my ears, be aware of the final experience.

Crouched on the bridge deck, cold and tired, the edge of my concentration blunted by fatigue, I passed into a trance-like indifference as the gale howled round me. Sometimes the moon would find a parting in the cloud and appear for a moment to give the wild scene a surrealist luminosity, briefly lighting the crazy world which surrounded me. Sometimes concentration would lapse or a sea would spring suddenly from nowhere, catch me unawares, and Iskra would ship heavy water. Then I would curse softly and work the pump until I heard it suck air. Once a violent breaking crest carried me towards overboard until I came sharply against the life-line. I became stiff with fatigue and the cold searched out my weakness.

The night seemed endlessly to prolong itself, staving off another day, as if the laws of the universe had been suspended. At midnight I was near the end of my endurance. I looked round with a shudder. It was an endless wilderness, unrelieved by any sympathetic feature, a confusion where nothing lived or stirred but anger and violence. Sometimes when Iskra was enclosed within a valley between the waves, I could look along the unbroken troughs in the half light radiated by the moon. The dark contours of the spent waves, their backs flecked with spume driven against them from the following crest, were gathering energy for the next release. Behind, the advancing mass would build up another unsteady mountain; at the moment of final imbalance it would totter over its own concave face, releasing its energy in a savage burst of power. The ocean was shrouded in a mist of blown spume. Each crest that Iskra mounted brought her into the full force of the wind. It was a solid thing, tearing and teasing and scratching as if it would wrench out her heart. The power of the wind numbed my senses. My vision was narrowed through salt-caked lids to the immediate perils mounting behind, each to be appraised and overcome in turn. From the crests the view was of an icy mountain range, jumbled and jostling peaks in eternal conflict, hurling themselves one against another.

I knew that I could go on no longer without rest. I had to get into the cabin, make myself a hot drink. My mind began to wrap itself round the idea until it assumed exclusive importance. I could feel the mug between my hands, taste the warmth of the liquid. I pumped Iskra dry, adjusted the steering vane, engaged the chain across its clamp on the tiller. I watched her carefully for ten minutes, undecided. She seemed safe. She would raise her stern against the walls of water and they would pass under her with a roar, the crests racing alongside, spending their energy harmlessly. As the sea passed she would slip down into the hollow, slewing herself to one side or the other, then the vane would tip in the wind, the tiller lines would force her back on course before the next crest was on her. The vane could do it as surely as I could for as long as the seas ran true. She was not going too fast, too slowly if anything without her tiny triangle of staysail, but the wind had now increased her speed. I would risk it. I would slip down, put on the kettle, come up again until it boiled, and then slip below again to make myself a cup of coffee. Watching her suspiciously, I slid open the companion hatch, unclipped my harness, climbed over the wash boards and went below. I saw from the clock that I had been steering for seven hours.

The cabin was the loveliest place I had ever been in. It was warm, it was dry, it was orderly after the confusion outside, it was home. I retrieved the kettle, filled it, found its whistle, fastened it on the stove and lit the gas. It flickered in the draught from the open hatch. I reached up and slid the hatch half shut. 'You'll be a good chap and give a nice whistle when you're ready for me.' I listened tentatively, sensing Iskra's movement. She was steady. I could leave her while I rested for a few moments. My circulation came tingling back, I began to feel warmth, I put my hands over the kettle, funnelling the warm air from the stove into my face. The noise of the sea was muffled inside the cabin; it seemed almost remote. I glanced at the barometer. It had reached a new low. I tapped it; the needle flickered but remained steady. This must be the beginning of the end - by morning it would ease. Damn it, I'd stay inside and have my coffee in luxury - she'd be alright for ten minutes. I got out a mug, fixed it in its fiddle on the table by the galley, reached in the locker for the coffee and spooned it ready in the mug. The kettle was beginning to steam.

I made the coffee, took the first sip. The hot liquid brought new life, I could feel it spread through my body, causing me to shudder. I must go on, I realised, if I stopped I would go to sleep, she would broach and all the effort would be wasted. I climbed back into the cockpit, the mug clutched in my hand. It would soon be morning. As I looked around the horizon I saw that the violence of the sea was dying down, the sky was lifting, the cloud breaking up. I saw a fleeting patch of blue to windward and I knew that I had weathered the storm. It would become, not like other storms, a memory, an experience, something that had passed over, leaving me and my Dolphin essentially as we had been before, but a new gauge to set against experience. It had displaced in my mind that other storm so many years ago in the Southern Ocean. I poured myself a glass of Don Felipe's brandy and drank a toast to my Dolphin.

IX

Bahamas Nightmare

I was not proud of my first lone voyage and was pleased enough to find an excuse to go again. I had survived it more by luck than by good management. When I looked back on it from the cool vantage of home, gazing out of my attic window across green fields and flowering trees, I realised that it had been a mess - an amateurish jaunt that I had been lucky to come out of with my life. I had not been prepared for solitude, and *Iskra* had not been properly prepared for a long single-handed voyage. I ought to have foreseen her tendency to broach-to in an ocean gale and to have had strong headsails that could not blow out; ought to have known from experience that she would be smashed by the seas if I allowed her to broach. I had inherited that old staysail from the previous owner and it had already served its time. It was a meanness that cost me dear.

I should have known that it was unacceptable to voyage across an ocean in a boat with no self-draining cockpit, open to the sea so that each time she shipped a wave it would flood the bilge and have to be pumped out by hand, making proper rest impossible and causing me to be exhausted when I should have been fresh. The engine should never have been allowed to become water-logged. If the tank fillers and air vents had been properly sealed it could have been used at any time to help her. An engine that doesn't work is a useless heap of iron.

Iskra leaked too much on that first voyage. I gave her a thorough refit and managed to make her as tight as any old wooden boat is likely to be. She was given new copper sheathing on her bottom, at great expense but worth it I believe, new keel bolts, rigging, a new skylight in a vain attempt to keep her free of drips inside the cabin. Her bottom was found to be in perfect condition when the old, paper-thin copper was peeled off. Her planking was as smooth, her seams as sound, her fastenings as bright as if she had been new. There was an old shipwright in the yard in Essex who had coppered yachts before and who knew the business. He made a faultless job of *Iskra*'s bottom so that when she stood on the slip ready for launching she was a wonderful sight - a newly minted coin, smooth and tailored like a dandy in a new suit, immaculate in her golden livery. My Dolphin was proud, his black fins and tail and his bananasplit smile reflecting this new glory. She was inspected by a Lloyd's surveyor and found to be in good order - in all respects ready for her third voyage to the Americas, to visit Tamarind on the occasion of her first birthday.

When the work was all done and the pain of paying for it had passed over, she lay at her mooring in Bradwell like a newly crowned queen, all bright paint, shining varnish, burnished brass. I had made her a canvas skin to fit inside her cockpit, with ample drains to take the water away and a new pump inside the cabin which would suck water from either bilge without my going outside to work it. I would make a better job of this new voyage, I thought, than I had of the last. Now that I was used to solitude I felt a compelling need for more of it.

I could have stopped with all honour satisfied, have stayed at home, attended to my business, supported my family, joined a respectable yacht club and kept *Iskra* as a monument to past glories. My Dolphin wouldn't let me. As *Iskra* lay to the quay through the long winters in her mud berth in front of the sail-maker's loft in Maldon, he bombarded me with his reproaches, flung shame at me whenever I appeared across the smooth grass. He is a creature of the free ocean, he wants none of sanity, of safety, of respectability. 'Get to sea,' he said; 'harbour rots good ships and good men.'

Iskra went to sea in all the finery of her refit in the late summer of 1974, bound for Nassau, Bahamas, on a date with Tamarind. This time I knew more of what to expect and had a better notion of how to deal with what the ocean and the gods would send me. I had learned something of how to keep myself from fatigue, I had gained a measure of calm in times of crisis, I was able to counter the whims and conceits that crowd the mind of a man alone. There would be no more swimming away from *Iskra* in mid ocean. I would try to make the voyage a model of careful planning and unhurried execution. I was learning to live with myself, learning to respect the constraints imposed by solitude. On this voyage I made fast passages and always arrived fresh and in good order.

Iskra sailed from the English Channel to Spain, cruised the coast of Galicia from Cape Ortegal to Vigo, sailed down the Portuguese coast and round Cape St. Vincent to visit a friend who lives in the Algarve, then to the Canaries where she visited all the islands except La Palma. I knew that Cuba was closed to me now. To re-visit Donna Dolores would only open old wounds better left untouched. Even if I had wanted to go to Cuba again I knew they would never allow such a voyage a second time. I would only be humiliated, told to leave without ceremony in spite of all the glory that had attended *Iskra*'s first visit. The Cubans never give reasons for their proscriptions - doors that were open become closed, leaving the caller to guess the reason.

I sailed across the Atlantic in twenty-three days. This time I went further south, left the voyage until later in the year and found better winds. It was unremarkable except for its smoothness and its absence of alarms. It is not difficult to sail down the trade winds in the right latitude and at the right season. Hundreds of yachts, big, small, good, indifferent, do it every year. It is the return voyage that weeds out the wheat from the chaff. The trades offer boundless peace and goodwill. For day on day the wind blows true and strong, bringing a feeling of timeless peace. This time I knew I could do it and I knew I could do it properly. I never wanted to share it with another person, it was my private delight; only my Dolphin could gauge the contentment of it. I recognised it as a supreme moment and thanked my stars that I was able to experience it.

Iskra came across the schooner *Integrity* on her Bahamas voyage. In Puerto Plata on my way through the West Indies I met a tall thin American called Bill who persuaded me to alter my plan and take him to Turks Island on my way to Nassau. Bill was a veteran helicopter pilot of the Vietnam War, shattered in his mind by two tours of duty. He had used his savings to establish a boat yard on Turks, at the southern end of the Bahamas chain of islands. When I met him he had been stranded in Puerto Plata after a fishing trip and wanted a lift back to Turks. There was no way for him to get back unless he could beg a ride on a passing ship or a yacht. I agreed to take him.

Bill was full of remorse and doubts about his part in the war. He talked about the war all through the night-and-day passage from Puerto Plata to Turks. I heard of its horrors first-hand for the first time. I got to know him well and we passed through a considerable adventure together - the towing of the schooner *Integrity*. Bill told me about the schooner in *Iskra*'s lamp-lit cabin as she sailed herself through the night. Neither of us could know that the schooner would occupy our minds and our bodies for the next month - enough to make a book about our adventure.

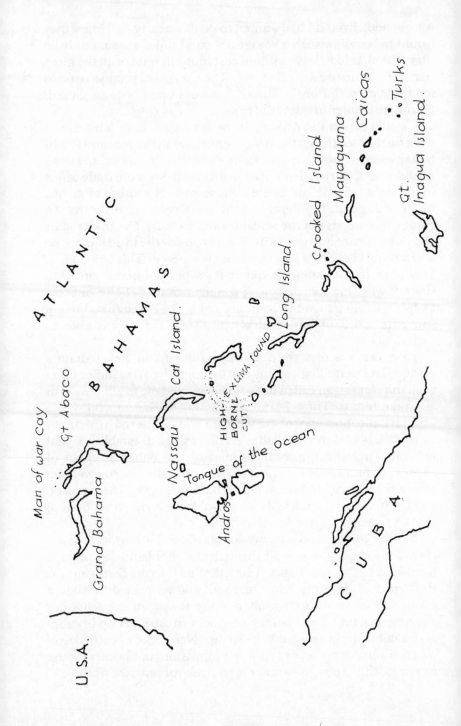

U.S.A.

Man of war Cay

Gt Abaco

Grand Bahama

A T L A N T I C

B A H A M A S

Cat Island.

Nassau

Tongue of the Ocean

Andros

HIGHBORNE CUT

EXUMA SOUND

Long Island.

Crooked Island

Mayaguana

Caicas

Turks

Gt. Inagua Island.

C U B A

114

The memory of sailing the 450 miles from Turks Island to Nassau still causes me to shudder. By luck, when I was in St Barts earlier in the voyage I was given an old and thumbed copy of the *Yachtsman's Guide to the Bahamas* and this, although out of date, sometimes inaccurate, even misleading, undoubtedly saved my life. Without it *Iskra* would have been smashed to pieces on any one of half-a-dozen reefs and my Dolphin would have found himself free to join his kind again. I had thought that this last, short part of my outward voyage would be easy. It proved to be a nightmare.

By the time I had finished with the *Integrity* I was on the way to being late for Tamarind's birthday. Instead of going back the way I had come and rejoining my original route through the Tongue of the Ocean, I thought I would save at least a day by sailing up the windward side of the islands, in the clear ocean and then into the Exuma Sound. There is a cut through the reef at the top of the sound which I thought I could find my way through with the aid of the *Guide*, then sail the fifty-odd miles across the coral bank to Nassau.

It would have been a good plan if I had not been alone. Sailing in the Bahamas is a special art demanding special skills. I soon found that the land, such as it is, can hardly be distinguished from the sea. Certainly at night it cannot be seen until you are on top of it. Having once seen it, there comes the problem of knowing which piece of land it is. It all looks the same - endless coral islands, all alike, all fringed with jagged reefs, sometimes close under the sea, sometimes breaking. At least three hands are needed to handle a boat in the Bahamas; one to keep a look-out, aloft from the cross trees, one to steer and read the chart and sailing directions, one to handle the boat.

I set sail in the evening from Turks, bound for Mayaguana Island where I would spend the next night. Most of the cays and islands are unlit, it would be safer to bring-up at night and sail only by day. In a strong wind and a rough sea I managed to get past the north shores of Caicos Island in safety and bring-up to a dubious anchorage in Mayaguan, where I spent a restless night watching *Iskra*'s anchor bearings in case she dragged. My first real fright came next day when *Iskra* nearly ran foul of French Cays, a pair of uninhabited and indistinguishable atolls between Mayaguana and Crooked Island.

I had plotted a course to give them a wide berth but had been set by a strong cross-current. The first I knew, the colour of the sea had changed from deep blue through aquamarine to a pale green and a line of surf stretched across *Iskra*'s bow in both directions. She was before a moderate gale with twin staysails set and the mainsail tied down to the boom gallows. I had seven minutes to stow the twins, set the mainsail and a jib and put *Iskra* on the wind. By luck the mainsail was already reefed. Even so, when she came round she put her rail under and laboured to windward, the pale, cruel seas sweeping over her. She scraped clear leaving the reef with its leaping surf and terrifying roar fifteen yards to lee'ard.

After that scrape I over estimated the current so that I passed clear of Long Island without seeing it. *Iskra* spent the night at sea, running downwind again with the same gale behind her. The next morning she had covered her distance by the log on what should have been a converging course with Long Island so as to pick up Cape St Marie, but I could see no land. I was getting tired and my judgement was fogged and unreliable. I saw land ahead, skirted by a reef and took it for Long Island. I altered course to starboard as the land began to open up ahead of me, puzzled because land kept appearing further and further to starboard.

I gazed at the chart until it swam before my tired eyes but it was an hour before I realised I was sailing along the shore of Rum Cay, nearly twenty miles to starboard. I cursed and swore at myself when the stupidity of this mistake came to me, put *Iskra* round and sailed almost back on my track to pick up the Cape. There was no possibility of getting proper sleep through this nightmare, no safe anchorage, no harbour I could make, no open sea with the peace and safety of space around me. I was in a trap and each mile I sailed took me further into it. Still the wind blew hard from the south-east.

I identified Cape St. Marie in the afternoon and *Iskra* entered the Exuma Sound. The Sound is a narrow bag in the ocean, 130 miles long, 30 miles wide, closed in by reefs except for an opening at the south of Eluthera, which leads back into the open ocean and a few cuts or gaps in the reef. *Iskra* entered the sound at the top between Cape Marie and Conception Island. The wind was still blowing a moderate gale straight into this bag and *Iskra* too was sailing inexorably into it at seven knots. In the night I took down all sail to slow her down. I read the log with the greatest care at Cape St Marie, my last certain landmark; the sea was unusually rough, even for so strong a wind, which was itself unusual for the time of year.

The next morning I could see nothing. I set twin staysails and continued into the bag. There was a lot of glare from the sun but not much visibility. I knew I would have to fix my position and identify the cut before mid-afternoon when the sun would be in my eyes and I would see nothing. When I had run the distance all but ten miles I took in the twins and set a reefed mainsail, altering course to the west so as to pick up the land.

At midday the reef appeared ahead - a line of breaking waves stretching as far as the eye could reach in both directions. Behind the reef I could make out the land, a low ill-defined shape of sand and coral devoid of any feature - no house, no tree, no hill; only the odd clump of what looked like coarse grass and an occasional undulation. The sailing directions spoke vaguely of huts and trees which I could see nothing of. *Iskra* ran her full distance and still I could see nothing tangible to get hold of for a fix. The leading

A line of breakers stretching as far as the eye could reach

marks for the cut were a tree and a wooden hut on the shore in line on a given bearing. Through the glasses I saw something that might fit, but no more so than half-a-dozen possible marks I had already seen that might fit.

A man up the mast would have been able to see over the surf - from *Iskra*'s cockpit I could see nothing. I sailed as close to the reef as I dared, the roar of it drumming in my ears. I hove *Iskra* to on the off-shore tack and scrutinized the shore with the glasses, alternately looking at the vague, inadequate drawing in the book. It had to be the cut - there was no other. I was almost at the end of the sound, I would have to get out of this or perish - from exhaustion if not from the reef. I put *Iskra* to the reef, let the sheet free and hurtled towards it. The towering surf came nearer - it roared like a wild, mad animal. A line of coral teeth showed momentarily as each wave broke, throwing a million particles of atomized water high in the air to form a cloud of blown spume which hung low over the reef. The marks were in line - it had to be right.

Iskra was racing towards it like a kamikaze warrior bent on his own destruction. Fright took hold of me - I must turn while I still had time, get out of it, put the helm down. Then I saw it, to port, a line of clear water between the walls of surf. She sailed into Highborne Cut and suddenly the sea was smooth. The passage turned to starboard again and suddenly she was through, suddenly out of the mad chaos of the reef, the agony of danger and fear and into a deep calm turquoise lagoon where all was quiet and peace. *Iskra* arrived in Nassau the day before Tamarind's birthday.

Nassau was full of my daughter's friends and therefore my friends. My Dolphin was made a fuss of, given a new coat of paint and his tail repaired where it had fallen foul of *Iskra*'s anchor chain. As in all these tropical heavens, I never felt at ease, was always anxious to be on my way. There is something artificial, removed from the real world, about Nassau and Antigua and Bermuda which makes me itch to be away whenever I am there. Everyone was hospitable and kind and generous towards me but I could not feel part of the place, could never identify with its struggles, disasters, triumphs because they were irrelevant and somehow false. Rich people are concerned with the flippancies of living rather than with life itself. Nassau palled after a few weeks. Having ascertained that Tamarind was really one year old and that the occasion was properly marked it was time to go home; I had achieved what I set out to achieve.

My Dolphin, for once in his life, had a weary look about him in spite of his new paint, as if he could use a spell of calm and quiet in England, resting his chin against the grass bank in the sailmaker's yard at Maldon. We set off for the north, crossed the North-East Providence Channel and passed through the reef again at Little Harbour, sailing through the Abacos in calm blue waters from coral island to coral island, from one perfect anchorage to the next, all protected by the same reef that had caused me distress. It was the happiest part of the voyage, always in good company, sometimes in delightful company from one spot to the next as far as Man of War Cay from where I made my departure for Bermuda.

The people of Man of War Cay were astonished that I should consider going out into the Bermuda Triangle alone - they were convinced to a man that there was something supernatural about the place, a belief I have always found it difficult to share. Certainly there are said to be some strange magnetic anomalies, which I have never experienced, and some fierce weather, which I have. *Iskra*'s survival gale on her Cuba voyage was in the Triangle and this Bahamas voyage she passed through another gale of nearly as great ferocity. This time both I and she were better equipped to cope with it.

We were in a different part of the ocean, well clear of the continental shelf of America, which made the seas more regular and even and therefore less destructive, although as big as in the previous gale. *Iskra* had a new storm staysail which gave me no worries, she had her patent canvas self-draining cockpit and she had an inside pump. These things, together with my greater knowledge of what was to come, put the experience on a different plane. This time I streamed a warp over the stern, which made an immediate difference to her and more as an experiment than as an exercise in survival, I used oil.

I used the long nylon warp I carry aboard which I had used for towing the schooner *Integrity*, paying out the bight, with an end fast to one side of the stern, untwisting the rope as it went over the side so that it was towed across the surface of the sea in a U-shape behind *Iskra*. It slowed her down and it calmed the seas behind her. They seldom broke and very little water came into the cockpit. I used oil when I began to get tired and wanted a meal and a sleep. I carry on board a one-gallon can of raw linseed oil. I made a tiny hole in the tin with the point of a nail - no more than a puncture, tied the tin to an old life jacket and towed the whole affair over the stern with a scope of about ten feet. At first nothing happened. After a few minutes a narrow slick appeared in *Iskra*'s wake, calming the sea like magic. I left it there until the gale moderated and then let the whole affair slip so as not to bring mess on board.

Apart from gales, I saw a phenomenon in the Bermuda Triangle on this passage which I have never been able to find an explanation for. It was a fine, calm day with a moderate, fair breeze. I saw a disturbance in the water about half a mile ahead. It looked like the tide race off Portland or Alderney on a rough day but here the depth of the ocean was 3,000 fathoms. The barometer was steady, there was no cloud. I sailed quite close to it, to within 200 yards, and looked at it through the binoculars. I could make nothing of it. There were no whales or fish that I could see, nothing untoward. I got scared and sailed away from it and saw it disappear. I cursed myself afterwards for not photographing it, which I could have done. When I mentioned this in Bermuda I could get no sense. 'Ah,' they said, 'all sorts of strange things happen in the triangle.'

The wreck of the *Girl Stella* had been robbed after it was brought up from the bottom of Porto Piqueran. Her clock and her barometer had been stolen from her cabin along with most of the odd bits and pieces of value that were inside her. I don't know whether it was the islanders of Flores who robbed her or a group of French skin-divers who were diving on the wreck. One item that went was a small painting of my first boat *Santa Lucia* that had been made by an old sailor I met on the Isle of Wight who took a fancy to her. I had paid him £5 for it. It was an oil painting on hardboard, a gem of its type, in a simple oak frame with no glass. I had a compulsion to go back to Flores on this voyage, see the wreckage of *Girl Stella* which I knew had been dragged up on the rocks and try to get back my painting. If I asked round the village of Santa Cruz, I thought, perhaps offering to buy the painting, someone might find it and give it back.

Iskra had an easy passage from Bermuda to the Azores, marked only by splitting her mainsail from luff to leech so that I had to stitch it across its width with palm and needle. A day running north of my course while I worked on the mainsail put me close

120

to Flores and I decided to go in and try to find my painting. I raised the island in the early morning and sailed close up under the southern point as I had before.

It was as it was, only I had changed. As I came up with the land the wind swung round to the north-east, as it had done before, but gently this time, with no malice in it. The place frightened me. It had a look of menace, of some secret malevolence which it would release like fierce guard dogs to trap me and tear me apart as soon as I was within its reach. I saw the little town, all quiet in the stillness of early morning - my courage faltered and I let the sheet free setting *Iskra* on course for Horta and feeling somehow humiliated by my cowardice. *Santa Lucia*'s painting would have to wait for a braver day.

Iskra came back to Bradwell from her Bahamas voyage without a mark on her, in all respects as she had been when she left. It was an easy, pleasant passage, fifteen days from Bermuda to the Azores and twelve days back to the English Channel. Even my Dolphin carried his new paint from Nassau back home without a mark on it. Boats are like people, it isn't work that bears them quickly to the grave but idleness. When a boat is being used she is being looked after; when she is laid up, or spends week after week swinging to her mooring, she is deteriorating. The rain lies in sly puddles on her decks and in the hidden corners of her coach roof, soaking in day by day without the pitch and roll of the ocean to throw it clear. The air under her transom, round the turn of her bilge and in the recesses of her stem and stern post becomes dank and putrid; weed and slime builds round her rudder, the sun dries out her hatches and skylights, her sails and cordage lie in constricting folds, wanting only to spread themselves to the fresh wind.

It is the same with me. I ache and creak and groan, bodily and in my mind, when I spend my days in city streets, pounding the hot pavements, creased into office chairs, robed in the fancy dress of convention. I become fat and weak and soft and fetid, sunk in shore-side sloth. My soul withers when the horizon shrinks to a few yards, my mind becomes smaller because it is concerned with small things, my spirit becomes mean, shut in by walls of convention and constraint. I lose my trust in people, I am out to do any man in the eye as I expect to be done in my eye, I become one of the rats in the rat race.

When *Iskra* came back from the Bahamas I really believed that I would swallow the single-handed anchor - I would make no more ocean voyages alone and there was no one with whom I could make an ocean voyage. I had done it all and I had proved everything that it was within my capacity to prove; to go again would be only to repeat, I could break no new ground. I had sailed out to see Tamarind on her first birthday. It would be trite to do it again on her second.

Now there was nothing for it but to content myself with my lot, to behave like everyone else in the real world behaves, to pull together what I had let go through my wanderings, to be done with philandering, to work at my table with a blank piece of paper in front of me. My Dolphin convinced himself that it was all over.

After many months of work the blank piece of paper turned itself into a book about the schooner *Integrity*. I persuaded my friend Martin that it would be profitable to publish it. I know I ought to do nothing but write magazine articles, which is a better-paid occupation than writing books and I ought to try to write for television. I don't like television, I don't much like magazines, and I do like books. I am old fashioned enough to feel reverence for a book. There is something splendid about a book, to have it in your hand, to flip the pages, to turn it this way and that, to dip in and read a paragraph here or there. To write a book and to see it published is a fine thing. I have written six books which have been published, several more which have not. The thrill of seeing them in print for the first time never palls. I have never actually seen anyone reading one of my books in the train but I have met people who tell me they have borrowed one from a friend.

Writing a book is an adventure. A book comes alive, leads the writer on with a life of its own so that he must follow as best he can. So far none of my books has had much success except, possibly, the last, *Single-Handed Cruising and Sailing*, which was the one I didn't want to write and didn't enjoy writing. After my first book *Terschelling Sands* the publisher went quietly into liquidation. I quarrelled with the publisher of my novel, *Rustler on the Beach*, through no fault of mine and he decided, not surprisingly, to have no further truck with me. Martin published my book about *Girl Stella*'s voyage to Cuba, *In Granma's Wake*. I met him in Hornfleur, or to be accurate, I met the rear end of him. The front end was under the counter of his old boat with a pan of hot pitch, trying

122

to stop some of her more obvious leaks. I recognised him at once as a kindred spirit.

Martin is a good publisher but he specialises in a field which is not my field so that he has a weak selling organisation for my type of book. Both the books that he published were moderately successful. All my books have been well reviewed and are well thought of, but this doesn't make them sell. The English have given up reading books unless their appetite is titillated by a massive advertising and press campaign, not available to me and Martin. But we knew that *Schooner Integrity* must sell in America - it is an American story about an American schooner. We had been unable to find an American publisher for it.

I don't know whether it was Martin or I who had the idea to fill *Iskra* with books and sail them to America. At first it seemed ridiculous. It was said as a joke over a pint of beer at lunch time and wasn't meant to be taken seriously but the idea was brilliant in its simplicity. I couldn't shake it off. I went on board *Iskra* where she lay in her winter quarters, all covered up, all her gear out of her, gently rising and falling on the tide, my Dolphin sound asleep until the spring. I measured the space where books could be stowed - under the bunk in the fo'c'sle, in my hanging locker for clothes, under the cabin floor in the turn of the bilge where there were wooden racks for food stowage, in place of the mattress in the for'ard sleeping berth.

Some gear would have to be left ashore - the spare mainsail, sun awnings, gear I had always considered essential for ocean cruising, gear that I had carried against dire emergencies that had never happened. All must be sacrificed for books. Books are heavy for their size, they take up a lot of space; above all they have to be kept dry. *Iskra*, in a gale in the ocean, is not a dry place. The books would have to be wrapped in polythene sheets and sealed with tape. The economics of selling books in America flitted round my mind as I sat in *Iskra*'s fo'c'sle. I began to see her as a floating bookshop, lying alongside the quay up and down the eastern seaboard of America with a big notice hanging on the shrouds, 'Books for sale - genuine Atlantic copies'. As I went ashore I shouted to my Dolphin, 'Wake up, we're going to America.'

This would be unlike any voyage *Iskra* had made before. Previously, she had always gone with the prevailing winds, down to the Canaries in the autumn, across the trade wind belt, winter in the tropics and back northabout with the westerlies the following spring. This time it would have to be different. I would leave England in the spring and be in America by mid-summer in order to sell the books in America during the sailing season. *Iskra* would cross the north Atlantic from east to west against the wind. It was a daunting undertaking for a fifty year-old gaff cutter. She has never been a windward sailing machine although she is no sluggard close hauled. I knew the punishment a boat must take sailing against the wind in the ocean and the punishment her crew must take.

There are three routes for a sailing vessel across the north Atlantic from east to west. The southern passes through Madeira and Bermuda and then follows the gulf stream north to the New England coast - too great a distance for *Iskra* to cover in the time available although it would avoid much of the bad weather. The northern route would be too cold, too rough and too long a distance between ports, but using the middle route I could sail to the Azores and then direct on the rhumb line to Newport, Rhode Island. There was another reason for using the middle route. I was in love.

I had parted from Celia, my family had melted away, as families do, and I had discovered Wendy. Put in such stark simplicity this sentence disguises a nightmare of doubt and uncertainty and guilt and unhappiness. I make no excuses or justifications for it. Love grows more potent with age, contrary to what might be expected. I have been more consumed by love, more ruthless in its pursuit, more careless of its consequences, more hurt by its cruelties and more fulfilled by its joys as I have grown older. Perhaps the knowledge that time has a limit, which no young person can recognise, makes me more anxious to exploit to the full the portion of it that is left. The craving for sex and love have always preoccupied my waking, sometimes my sleeping thoughts to the exclusion of most other things. The craving is a kind of burden that has to be carried through life with occasional, sometimes long, periods when it has been satisfied. The periods when it has not been satisfied have been barren and hard to bear. Now that I have settled the whole affair by my attachment to Wendy I don't have to worry about it any more, which is a great relief. She feels the same sense of relief.

By taking the middle route across the Atlantic *Iskra* would pass through the Azores and Wendy would be able to take a holiday from her job and come out by plane. One day she would come with me on a long voyage across an ocean, or perhaps not. Half of her wanted to, half of her was frightened. At that time she could not, because of her work, which was important to her and in any case, we needed the money she earned. This made no difference to love.

I went back to Martin and said, 'I'll risk the voyage if you'll risk the books'. He agreed. Martin is an unusual type of publisher. He delivered 400 *Integrity* books alongside *Iskra* in Maldon and I wrapped them up, sealed the packets with tape and stowed them below. I took another 400 of my novel *Rustler on the Beach* which I bought from the publisher to save them from the junk shops. Together they were worth £3,000 at their face value.

I would not have woken my Dolphin from his sleep in this manner and persuaded him out into the ocean again without good reason. I knew the *Integrity* book was a good book - I would have thought so even if it had been written by someone else. I knew it must have a sale in America. It had flopped in England not because it had deserved to but because of the nature of the

book market and the changed reading habits of the English. The comparative excellence of television in England has all but crushed the market for ordinary good reading, which a few years ago could have expected moderate to good circulation. People who write these books have been squeezed on to the dole. Now there are fewer books and more potential writers. In America, I reasoned, television is not as good as in England and does not catch the attention and imagination of book readers; my book about an American schooner should have a chance there. A good way to test the theory was to take the books to America and try. If I succeeded in selling them I believed I would soon find an American publisher. The novel *Rustler on the Beach* I wasn't so sure about but I had a feeling that Americans would like it. My feeling was justified.

I have never crossed the ocean without a valid reason for doing so; I don't believe in or have any interest in stunts. Essentially, I cross the ocean in my boat in order to arrive on the other side and on this occasion, particularly, I had a good reason for doing it. Perhaps in America I would be able to revive my flagging fortunes as a writer. The politics of it, which had deterred me before, are now irrelevant. Vietnam is history, its horror has been superseded by other horrors, making it clear that no nation has a monopoly of horror, that any one of them can be as evil as any other. There was a new atomic horror in fashion at the time that was all-embracing, rendering every other issue meaningless. Now there is the ultimate horror of pollution and global warming.

X

Up the Pole

In the spring of 1980 Wendy and I sailed round the English coast from Bradwell, where *Iskra* lives when she is not laid up in Maldon, to Dartmouth, in easy stages, weekend by weekend. *Iskra* was immensely heavy with her cargo of books in addition to stores for a prolonged cruise, down to her marks and almost to the top of her copper sheathing which when she is light, rides six inches above the water. As we sailed her together I began to understand that I was no longer devoted to being alone; the easy comradeship, the fun, the subtle exchange of sympathy was something I hadn't experienced for years. My Dolphin accepted Wendy as a new companion with great delight. She has a fund of love for all creatures through the entire range, elephants to tiny insects, even creatures made of cloth or wool or rags or wood. My Dolphin came under the umbrella of her compassion. I chose Dartmouth as my port of departure because the river is beautiful, the anchorage secure, good fresh stores are plentiful and because South Dartmouth, Massachusetts, was where the *Integrity* was built. A voyage from Dartmouth to Dartmouth should help to sell books.

Wendy made me buy a VHF radio so that I could report my progress to passing ships and send messages to her to relieve the worry of this first voyage I had made since I knew her. Now that we were in this business together things were not as straightforward as they had been. When she left after a week in Dartmouth and I watched her train pull out of the station I was clutched by an unfamiliar and overriding grief. My world suddenly emptied itself, my confidence in my ability to withstand the ocean alone evaporated. When I watched her diminishing hand waving out of the train window I knew I would have to stop sailing alone. I hurried from the station back to *Iskra* and went straight to sea before my resolve evaporated.

It was a slow, frustrating, sometimes tedious voyage to Ponta Delgada in the Azores. It started with two gales in the entrance to the English Channel and continued with contrary winds and calms. At one time it looked as if we were taking too long, so that Wendy would be in Ponta Delgada first, pacing the harbour wall, worried out of her reason. Only one of the ships I saw either could or would send a message back to Lloyd's and that was near the beginning when *Iskra* was hardly clear of the English Channel. I became worried because I knew she was worried. When the weather was nice I wanted her to be there, when it was foul I was glad she wasn't.

Like the Mate of a tramp steamer watching his cargo I fussed over the books, inspecting them every day, covering them with extra layers of polythene when the seas came aboard and always keeping *Iskra* pumped dry so that bilge water would never reach the books that were stowed under the bunks. *Rustler on the Beach*, which I had paid a modest amount for, were under the bunks and the *Integrity* copies were packed well clear of the bilge, in prime dry stowage space in the fo'c'sle. Whenever it was fine I rigged a wind chute over *Iskra*'s for'ard hatch to induce air circulation round them.

I was fourteen days on a passage that should have taken no more than ten. By the time I arrived and telephoned her Wendy had convinced herself that I was drowned. She came by plane two days later. We spent ten perfect days together in Ponta Delgada, swimming in the warm sea, exploring the island of Sao Miguel, meeting the strange collection of people who inhabited the yachts homeward bound to Europe - to France, Holland, England, Portugal, Germany. None were going to the west against the wind. I believe they all thought I was either ignorant or had taken leave of my reason. The holiday led to another heart-breaking moment when Wendy went back to England. Again, I went straight to sea before I could change my mind.

Iskra sailed 2,181 miles from Ponta Delgada to Newport, Rhode Island in thirty-four days, mostly against strong westerly winds. She suffered no damage which I was not able to repair myself. I lost one and a half stone in weight.

Wendy came to Newport a week after I arrived. She said I was edgy, meticulous and fussy about the boat, not allowing her to do anything - boil an egg, fold a sleeping bag, dry the dishes - unless it was done exactly as it had been done in the ocean. Everything had to be put away in exactly the same place, each fork and knife the right way round in the cutlery tray, each coffee cup in its exact spot. The routine had driven so hard into my mind that it had displaced all commonsense, had paralysed my ordinary tolerance. After she had been with me for a few days I found myself telling her how to make bean stew - she who is the best cook that has ever been in my world. Then I realised that there was something wrong with me. It took the three weeks which was her holiday before I was sane again.

It wasn't surprising that I should have been affected. It was a gruelling thirty-four days. At times I was driven to the borders of insanity by frustration and fatigue, in spite of the lessons I had learned, or thought I had learned, on other voyages. At times I was so fatigued I groped my way round the boat like a zombie, unsure from one moment to the next what I was supposed to be doing. The west wind blew for week on week, shredding my nerves, tearing at the edges of my reason until I wondered whether the torment of it would ever end. The lowering sky, close over the mast, enclosed my world in a shroud of grey; sea and sky merging one into the other along a dim and misty horizon. For days the sun never penetrated. When it did, my world was flooded with unfamiliar brilliance so that I blinked and puckered my face with astonishment, like an animal waking to the daylight after a winter's hibernation. Everything I possessed became wet through drips in the coach roof, the blown salt spray and the general dampness which pervaded everything. *Iskra* flogged through it all at an average speed of 64 miles a day.

The first day was the best. She ran 128 miles with a breeze from the north which I expected, leaving the lovely island behind in fine style and convincing me that I would make a fast passage. Then the weather fell light with variables, sometimes from the north, sometimes the southeast but usually, however light, from a direction that allowed Iskra to point the course. For eight days I nursed her to the west, using the engine in short bursts, taking advantage of any puff that would serve to push her a mile on her way. It was slow and hard work but I always knew that it would be slow. In the first ten days I managed to cover 790 miles. Then the wind went to the west and stayed there until *Iskra* reached the Gulf Stream, except for one day when it blew fresh from behind and I set her twin staysails.

I believe it was an astonishing performance for a fifty-two year-old boat, a flog to windward for more than 1,000 miles in the ocean. My Dolphin put on his look of obstinacy and determination, like a marathon runner or a climber; he put his head down, wiping out his happy smile for twenty days. For most of the time *Iskra* was reefed; for much of it she laboured under her storm trysail and staysail, as much sail as would be carried by a dinghy on a fine afternoon. The distance she sailed through the water was two-thirds more than the distance along the rhumb line. To achieve her average sixty-four miles a day she sailed a minimum of 100 miles a day through the water, taking account of a few days of fair wind, or days when the wind veered or backed from the west enough to allow her to point the course. In addition she was punching a contrary current of up to one knot. I began to wonder how she could go on taking the punishment. I had to sail her free, with the sheets started, otherwise she would have shaken and banged herself to pieces.

I used to sit inside listening to her as she toiled into the wind, picking herself up and thrusting herself through the contrary waves. I expected to see her planking spring away from the stem, her decks buckle under the strain, her coach roof cave in as ton after ton of water fell on it. I expected to see her sails split as the unceasing, nagging wind tore at the stitches; the shackles that fasten her shrouds to the chain plates spring apart, her sheets and halyards give up and loose their hold. In the end it wasn't my Dolphin or *Iskra* or her valiant and faithful gear that weakened - it was me.

A man can drive a boat downwind; he can put on a crush of sail, flog her and bash her until she breaks if he wants to. Against the wind it's a different story, the boat is master here. She has more strength than any man alone. She will wear him down, reduce him in size, take the conceit out of him unless he reaches an accommodation with her. She will wage a physical and psychological battle against him until he grants her the measure of ease and safety she needs if she is to survive and continue. A man who tries to force more from a boat than she is prepared to give will, in the end, destroy himself. A boat has a natural gait when sailing to windward across an ocean and the man who is her partner in the affair must find it and keep to it. If I tried to crowd sail on *Iskra* and point her too close she would begin to drip and leak, making of life a discomfort that no man could stomach. She would wince and groan as she forced herself against the waves and the wind, crying out with such shrill complaint that no person could gainsay it. She would hurl herself sideways and up and down with such violence that no man could live inside her. In the end I would ease her off the wind a point, or reef her or change to her storm trysail, or reef the storm trysail and then she would quieten down as a nervous horse will respond to a generous-minded rider. She never stopped, I never hove her to, but she insisted on justice, on what was right for her. My Dolphin was in league with her. The set of his expression turned to a scowl if I tried to abuse her.

On the tenth day I realised I still had 1,400 miles to go to Newport. *Iskra* had made thirty-six miles the previous day. Now she was becalmed but, for the first time, there was a long, easy swell from the west. It told me what I didn't want to know - that I was in the westerlies. Any wind from now on would be from ahead. *Iskra* rolled and wallowed in the swell so that I had to take the sails down to save them from chafe. As soon as I had them down a tiny breeze would come and I would haul them up again. It was doldrum weather without the slashing rain squalls, the bright sunshine and crisp white clouds, without the flying fish. She would sail for a few minutes and then the wind would leave her again, the sky sultry, overcast. It was hot, oppressive.

It went on in this manner for three days. When I tried to sleep she would go off course and point herself back to England. I was tired, irritated, short of temper. I had only seen one ship, nearly a week back which had taken a message for Wendy over the VHF machine. I had been swimming over the side, not for pleasure but to refresh my body. Now I was frightened of it, staying close under the bowsprit as if my Dolphin would protect me and always scanning the ocean for some hint of danger. Being in the sea seemed to reduce me in size, shrinking me and taking away my courage. *Iskra* was vast, towering above like a ship, her sides all smooth and slippery so that I doubted whether I would ever climb aboard.

The log line got itself twisted round the skeg of the steering vane and turned itself into a tight ball of twists and kinks, impossible to unravel. It had fouled the propeller and broken itself near the rotator. As I towed it astern to free it from kinks the bare end slipped through my hands and was gone overboard, leaving me with the rotator and no line. One of my more senseless economies - I only had one log line on board. I cried out in despair and anguish into the empty spaces. I could only calm myself by writing down what had happened in my journal. I improvised another line but the log never registered accurately for the remainder of the passage. Then the first south-westerly gale came. It was a relief.

There were five gales, all from the south-west. They may not have been severe gales, I have the wind force recorded in the log as force 8 for each of them, but every yachtsman's judgement of wind force is subjective. They were against me and therefore they may have seemed stronger than they were. Each time *Iskra* was reduced to her reefed staysail and reefed storm trysail. In one of them I discovered that she would continue to sail against the wind without the trysail, with only her tiny triangle of staysail flying. I would have expected her to have turned and fled from the wind under this rig but she contrived to plough slowly and doggedly ahead at an angle of fifty-five degrees to the wind - a remarkable quality. Each gale drove her far to the north and after each one the wind would veer, sometimes right round the clock to the south-west again over the space of two or three days and I would recover distance to the south.

Once it settled in the east for a few hours. I set *Iskra*'s twins for the first and only time on the passage and experienced the heady elation of a trade wind run. But it never was a trade wind. I knew it wasn't, I knew it couldn't last and it didn't. If it was enough for me to get my trousers dry I was happy, *Iskra* dripped relentlessly through her cabin top, another economy. In her re-fit after the Cuba voyage I had told the yard to leave the cabin top - I would patch it up with paint and gunge. I spent hours patching it and always the leaks found a new route. On this voyage there was a drip that came over my head as I stood at the galley cooking - a refinement of Chinese torture. The lee bunk was a miniature shower bath with one drip directing itself with uncanny aim into my ear. I rigged a canvas bunk-board to stop myself from falling out and slept in the weather bunk, like a goat on the side of a mountain.

The messages to Wendy kept me going - without them I believe I would have died of depression. Curiously they came exactly at one week intervals. After a week was up a ship would come by, almost to the day. Sometimes they were great tankers which steamed past without seeing *Iskra*. I would call them on the VHF, I would flash them with the Aldis light, I would fly the flag signal ZD2, I would even shout across the ocean in despair, all to no avail. But, invariably, after a week a ship came that I could contact. Sometimes they answered me on Channel 16 as soon as I called; sometimes I would flash 'VHF radio' with the lamp, the penny would drop and they would come through. They always agreed to send my message to Lloyd's, giving *Iskra*'s position so that Lloyd's could telephone the message to my office and so to Wendy. The effect on me was electric.

A ship that passed by without seeing me, refusing to respond to the radio, the lamp or my flag signal, left me in a state of profound depression. I felt like the last person on the surface of the earth, shunned, humiliated, abandoned. The ship that took my message for transmission to Lloyd's left me in ecstasy; laughing, shouting out happy greetings to the empty air, feeling that all men were my brothers. To know that Wendy knew that I was safe and well, however slow the passage, made me feel that everything in the world was in order. The effect of the messages on Wendy was just as powerful. If no messages came she would build fantasies of disaster in her mind which fed themselves on silence until she was almost in mourning for me. On the first passage from Dartmouth when she received only one message she was distraught with worry while I was safe with calm seas and blue skies. On the second part when I was in some danger and much discomfort she was serene with her weekly messages which she would plot on the Atlantic Ocean page of her old school atlas.

Things began to go wrong, not singly, but all at once; minor things which in themselves I would take in my stride but which assumed importance out of all proportion because of the conditions. One night the working jib split across near the top. I heard it flapping, dressed up in wet gear, put on my harness, climbed to the spray-swept foredeck, looked round behind the staysail and saw a patch of dark sky through the sail. I got it in off the end of the bowsprit and set a larger jib in its place - the only sail I had to replace it. But the wind was freshening and the big jib was really too much for her. As I stitched in the light of an oil lamp I could feel her begin to pound and crash against the increasing waves. The usual thin line of bilge began to appear along the lee side of the cabin, encroaching over the floor as she rolled. I would have to pump her out - she always had to be kept dry or the books would be sodden - the *Rustlers* stowed under the bunks were within inches of the bilge water when she was heeled.

I put down my palm and needle and walked across the cabin floor to the cockpit. Suddenly I slipped, both my feet flew away from under me and I landed heavily and painfully on my side. The floorboards in the cabin were all slippery, like ice. Then I could smell diesel - there was a leak somewhere; diesel had dripped into the bilge and the bilge water had left a film of oil

133

over the floor boards. I went into the cockpit and started to work the pump. After a few strokes the handle and the shaft came right out of the pump housing - 'Christ, oil all over the books'. The inside pump wasn't working, it needed a new lead through the bilge - bloody economy again. The sail was in a heap in the cabin. It would get covered in oil. The wind was freshening, she needed reefing. She dipped her bow and scooped up a heavy sea which rolled over the cabin top, cascading across the deck, tumbling into the cabin through the open hatch and wetting my last dry pair of trousers. I would have changed places with any man going home on the 5.42 with his bowler hat and his rolled umbrella.

The sky was black, the barometer falling again. 'Why are we bedevilled by bad weather?' I asked my Dolphin. It was the summer time when the sun shines, the air is full of zephyr breezes, the white clouds meander across the blue fields of heaven. Did he have no pull, no influence, no power that could persuade the weather to smile? He never relaxed his tense, grim expression. 'We're in this together.' he seemed to say to me. 'Forget self-pity - get on with it.' He was right. I put *Iskra* about and dried her with the electric pump which takes from the port side of the bilge. The discharge left a long narrow slick behind her. The fuel tanks were leaking - I'd lose my diesel. I went back to my stitching, treading gingerly across the cabin floor, sickened by the smell of diesel. Soon it would be morning; I would need daylight to change jibs again. The stitches progressed across the sail infinitely slowly, first one side of the seam, then back the other way. When it was done I looked over the sail, found another seam that was weak.

When I had finished the blackness of night had become the greyness of day. The foredeck of a small yacht in rough weather is a bleak place. *Iskra* has no pulpit, no rail, only the forestay to give a hold. The mesh of ropes, halyards, bowsprit outhaul, sheets, must be unravelled and then re-made to change a jib. The bow leaps and plunges. Sometimes a sea rolls over, wrenching at my feet, striving to prise me free, shake me off, wash me away. I set my eyes and my concentration to the job - every move, every shift of hand or foot, every grip thought out against some error which might cost me a ducking or an accident or the loss of a piece of gear. I am frightened to look around at the bleak ocean for fear the clutching emptiness will take away my resolve. My Dolphin lives here, he is part of it, joined to it by nature, I am a stranger, perhaps an imposter. I sigh with relief and the lifting of fear when I regain the cockpit and the reassuring, welcoming hatch when the job is safely done. What is it that makes me love this lonely world I inhabit?

The oil had leaked out of a spare can stowed low down under the cockpit floor, which with the endless motion, had rubbed against a sharp corner of the engine mounting until a tiny hole let out the diesel. *Iskra*'s engine had never done me a bad turn before this - our relationship is one of pure love, unsullied by any cross moment. We are a honeymoon couple on the ocean. *Iskra*'s previous owner had told me the engine was useless and unusable but from the moment I saw it I knew he was wrong, knew that we were going to be friends. It is not as old as *Iskra*; it was built in 1939, a two-cylinder Ailsa Craig with a massive iron flywheel that revolves at a stately 600 revs a minute. If its fuel is clean it never fails to start, provided I can turn it over fast enough. It runs with a timeless, even thump, giving out an aura of sturdy reliability. It doesn't make *Iskra* go fast but I am not often in a hurry. A modern engine would be a quarter of the size, would give twice the power, would be expensive to buy and would be nothing but a trouble to me.

My meanness in this instance as in some others, has paid off. It is no bad thing to be mean; the art of it is to know when generosity is better business than meanness. It took a morning to clean the oil out of the bilge with detergent. The gale I had expected didn't mature beyond a strong wind, giving me leisure to mend the pump. It too is old - it was fitted when *Iskra* was built in 1930 and I believe it had never been taken to pieces before except to replace the washer. A retaining pin at the bottom of its shaft had sheared, allowing the shaft slowly to un-thread itself until it parted company with the plunger, leaving the plunger at the bottom of the pump housing. It was all made of solid bronze and brass. In half a day I was able to get it out of its housing and using the vice in the fo'c'sle and a blowlamp I carry, I dismantled it, repaired it and put *Iskra* back on the starboard tack. I took all the books out from under the bunk and carefully wiped the polythene packets.

The weather waged a relentless war of nerves. After three weeks at sea we were on the fringes of the Gulf Stream and the depressions came in thick and fast. I knew they would come, the Admiralty pilot book told me but I wasn't prepared for their ferocity or for the ferocity of the contrary current. The pattern repeated itself endlessly; heavily overcast, rain, a strong or gale force south-west wind for a day or two, easing and veering to north-west then north, when the sun would come out briefly, then quickly round to south, with a calm for half a day and thick fog. Then back to south-west, the fog usually continuing until it started to blow hard again. It happened with predictable and remorseless regularity and it began to wear my resistance thin. Sometimes there were electric storms of great intensity, the rain pouring out of the sky so heavily that it was painful to go on deck, the lightning flashing and sparking and spluttering in terrifying and at the same time fascinating displays, so that I watched them mesmerised, half frightened and half glorifying in the extraordinary power of it, the jagged forks striking within feet of *Iskra*. I made fast a length of wire to the bottoms of each of the topmast stays and dropped them overboard with a weight, in the ineffectual hope of routing the lightning into the sea if the mast were struck.

On day twenty-four, before dawn, I was woken by a bang that shook every rivet in the ship. She shook so that the kettle rattled on the stove, the lamps jumped in their gimbals, the chart dividers clattered out of their stowage. I thought she had hit some solid object and would immediately sink. I ran to the cockpit. There was a big sea running, water was all over the deck and the coach roof; a fitful moon blinked briefly between scudding cloud showing the bleak, hostile ocean tumbling towards us in endless avalanche. I could see nothing wrong. She must have struck the side of a wave, catching it against the flat side of her bow as it rose to the peak of its power. I felt a sudden surge of sympathy for her. 'You poor old bastard,' I said to her softly, 'it's wrong to put you through this.'

I began to work the pump automatically, always fearful for the books. There seemed to be a lot of water in her - more than I would have expected. I suddenly became convinced that she was sinking. The wind dropped to nothing, leaving her to hurl herself from side to side in mindless fury, the boom and the gaff crashing over every time she rolled to bring up against the sheet with a shudder. The sky went black; I glanced at the barometer, it was down five millibars from the last entry in the log. I started the engine more to keep her steady and pointing towards where we were going and to give me occupation than for the miniscule progress it would achieve. I quickly packed a survival bag to take

136

with me in the liferaft; a can of water, flares, glucose tablets, nuts and raisins, a shirt, trousers and a hat, my money, passport, the ship's papers. Then the engine developed a leak in its exhaust between the block and the cooling water box and I had to stop it and take the sails down.

The exhaust system has never been included in my blanket feeling of love for the engine. It is a kind of mother-in-law figure. I forgot about the leak while I mended the exhaust, stripping off the insulation and wrapping the fractured pipe with a patent bandage which I carry for the purpose. By the time it was done the wind came back from the north-west, the sky began to clear and the leak, astonishingly, disappeared. I wonder now whether there ever was a leak or perhaps *Iskra* was outraged when she was struck so hard and leaked for a spell to show her displeasure.

Sometimes the Gulf Stream would turn against *Iskra* and run with such force that she was taken back on her tracks. On two consecutive days I saw brief breaks in the cloud and was able to snatch a sight in the morning and another at noon. It was a hazardous business standing up on the stern, wedged against the boom gallows, my sextant, which I value above any other single item of equipment on board *Iskra* clutched in my right hand, my safety harness clipped to the lifeline, a stopwatch round my neck. Sometimes the sun was behind the sail and *Iskra* would have to be turned off the wind. She would career off downwind with a bone in the Dolphin's mouth thinking she had been graced with a fair wind, losing ground to lee'ard that it would take hours to recover, while I struggled to balance a dancing, leaping sun on a jagged horizon, eclipsed every few seconds by the breaking crest of some monster ocean wave.

At the best of times it is hard to get an accurate sight from a small boat when the height of eye is no more than eight feet - at the worst of times it is a miracle. Yet my sights were remarkably accurate. Each time I spoke a ship to send Wendy a message they would give me a position from their electric navigation machine and each time my observed or estimated position was within a mile of it. If conditions were good I would take two sights, one after the other and work them separately; in bad weather I might be lucky to snatch one. I use an archaic method of working my sights, which I learned when I first went to sea countless years ago. It serves me well enough. Once the sight is taken and on the stop-watch, comes the task of getting myself and the sextant back into the cabin without a soaking. One day I slipped and fell heavily into the cockpit, bounced off the rail and tumbled down with the sextant held above my head. I thought I had broken a bone - I hadn't and the sextant was safe.

The Gulf Stream funnels out from the Florida Strait and then fans itself out across the Atlantic. Along its southeastern edge it develops spines of back-current which curve away from the main stream and sweep round and back on themselves with considerable force. On day twenty-four, which is engraved on my mind, the day the weather set in to be as unpleasant as it knows how to be, I took my sights and found *Iskra* twenty miles back on her direct reckoning position. I thought I might have made a mistake in my calculations but could find none. Then I thought that conditions had been so bad when I took the sights that I had made massive errors in both of them - I would believe anything rather than that she was back on her track. The next day conditions were still bad but I took the sight with the greatest care, almost falling overboard and almost drowning the sextant in spray. This time she was further back still.

The character of the sea in the Gulf Stream was extraordinary. It seemed to be a different colour, a kind of dull puce. It was leaping about all over the place, forming itself into lumps without true form or direction. I worked the sights over and over again, not wanting to believe their message, but could find no error. I had been carried backwards and to the south by a current, far out in an ocean. I found mention of 'freak back-currents' in the Admiralty Pilot and I afterwards confirmed it in America. It has been measured and documented by the U.S. Hydrographic Office; the spines are now predicted and information is given about their antics on American radio, small comfort to my shattered spirits even if I had known about it. I had to accept that *Iskra* had made less than twenty miles in two days of hard sailing.

When we are down we usually get hit. 'I am beginning to be depressed,' I wrote in my journal, 'I must pull myself out of it.' I had just been knocked off my balance, standing at the galley making coffee. I had fallen on the cabin sole, spilling hot coffee over the chart table, the starboard bunk, the galley stove and all over myself, including my face. I wept with rage and frustration. I was worried, fatigued. I wrote a list in my journal, first of everything that was wrong for me and next of everything that was right. I found on the credit side, that I had plenty of food, still some fresh onions and potatoes, plenty of water, one of *Iskra's* fifty-gallon tanks was still full, I knew my position to within a few miles. I was near the American coast - too far to the north but I had a chart and a list of radio beacons. I could already hear, faintly, the powerful radio beacon on Yarmouth, Nova Scotia.

Iskra was still in good order, nothing serious had broken. The weather was all that was wrong and that, in the end, would probably reverse its unpleasant face. All the same, I was down. It was almost a week since I had spotted a ship; Wendy would be worried. My Dolphin still wore a look of sullen, morbid disenchantment with the whole undertaking. Then I was hit.

Bernard Shaw believed that only fools learn by experience - the wise don't have the experience because they are cunning or careful enough to evade it. Experience only teaches what we ought already to know. But experience leaves something of value behind with us, if not wisdom at least an understanding which it is difficult to obtain without it. I would not wish to be without the recollection of what happened to me on that same day twenty-four although it came near to taking my life.

The wind eased in the afternoon and I hoisted the mainsail again. The routine is ground into me, hoist both halyards together, when the throat is two blocks belay them both, sweat up the throat, make it fast, coil it down, then hoist the peak until the sail is nicely trimmed. I was hoisting the peak when I felt it give, jerk, then take up. I belayed the fall, walked to the weather side and when I looked aloft I perceived at once what had happened. The block on the gaff had let go, its wire strop had broken and it was now hanging against the mast. When I lowered the sail the block would stay there, up above the crosstrees. I would have to go aloft to get it down. For as long as the sail was up and the wind light all would be well but once it began to blow again, the strain on the gaff, held only by one part of the halyard, would be unacceptable. Then it would be difficult to take the sail down or reef it and impossible to hoist it again. At first I thought I might get away with it. I only had 300 miles to go and it might stay calm so that I could leave the mainsail up for the rest of the voyage. Then I reflected on the experience of the past week and I knew that I would have to climb aloft, pull the block to the deck and fasten it to the gaff again with a new strop.

I have often been aloft before without difficulty, but not in the Gulf Stream. It is easy enough on the mooring in some quiet creek, or even at sea on a calm day but here everything was different. Even in a light wind *Iskra* would run into patches of confused sea, generated by the current, when she would hurl herself dementedly, pitching and rolling at the same time. It was hard to stand on the deck but I knew that once up the mast I would be thrown from side to side like a toy monkey on a stick. I took the sail down with a sick feeling of disquiet and got ready to climb the mast.

I found the bo'sun's chair, stowed at the bottom of a locker under a mountain of spare gear that had been displaced from the fo'c'sle by books, I started the engine and left it running slowly. With a little way on she would be quieter. I hooked the chair to the throat halyard, I would be able to reach the block from the top of it. I made sure I had my knife with me, on a lanyard round my neck. I shackled the top of the chair to a shroud; this would help to stop me from swinging like a pendulum and crashing against the mast. The shackle would slide up the stay as I went up.

I got into the chair and began to haul myself aloft. As soon as I was above the deck *Iskra* seemed to come alive. Every movement she made was multiplied in its violence as I went higher. At ten feet above the deck the chair wound itself round and round the stay - it took ten minutes to unwind it. I gained height in spasms, waiting for a moment when she was still to pull frantically on the halyard. My legs and arms were squeezed between the shrouds and the chair, raising red, painful weals. At fifteen feet the shroud converged with the mast and I was dashed against it with astonishing force. Every wire stay I clung to was wrenched out of my hand, the other hand held the fall of the halyard. I gained height inch by inch, getting tired fast. By the time I got to the cross trees I was nearly exhausted. I was shaken by the movement like a rat in the jaws of a terrier, lacerated where the wire stays cut into my legs and arms, bruised where I had been hurled against the mast. Then I saw that the chair was foul - I couldn't move it any higher because the fall of the topping lift was behind it, stopping it from moving further up. 'Fuck,' I said. No one answered. I tried to undo the shackle and free the chair but I couldn't get it undone. I looked up - the block was six feet above my head.

If I had been a wiser seaman I would have given up, come down the mast, thought the job through and then tried again.

But I am not. If I were more sensible, less pigheaded, I would not be there in that ocean. I have a streak of obstinacy which will not allow me to stop doing something I have started until I have finished it. Sometimes it's a good streak, sometimes it isn't.

I decided to make the chair fast, climb out of it, stand on it and so reach the block. I doubled the fall of the halyard round the top of the chair and put a half hitch in it. Then I struggled upwards, holding on to the mast and crosstree. When I tried to stand on the chair it wobbled and shot away from under my feet so that I almost fell. Then I got my feet on it and stood up. As high as I reached, my hand was inches below the block. I climbed out of the chair and stood on the crosstree. 'Got you, you bastard.' I pulled the block down, paused for a second to look round, standing on the crosstree, clinging for my life to the mast. It was overcast; if anything the sea was more lumpy. As *Iskra* rolled and pitched I looked down on the waves, then the deck with its untidy confusion of ropes and sails swung across the screen of my vison, then the sea the other side, the same uneven brownish purple, inverted like a crazy upside-down film strip.

I started to climb back into the chair. It had got itself turned round and round the shroud again, but this time with the fall of the halyard twisted up with it. I could reach it with my foot from where I stood on the crosstree. Each time she rolled to starboard I managed to kick the chair and persuade it to unwind itself a turn. By the time I got it free I was beyond what I had previously thought of as a state of exhaustion. Somehow I got myself back into it, through the tangle of ropes that now held it in a kind of cocoon. Now all I had to do was to untie the fall of the halyard and lower myself down again. Soon it would be over. Now I was being thrown about more because I no longer had the strength to steady myself. I no longer cared as long as I got down to the deck again. I slipped the halyard and began to lower. Slowly the chair descended. Then it stopped and I couldn't shift it down another inch. I looked below me - the fall of the halyard had wound itself round one of *Iskra*'s sidelight screens and was as securely fast as if I had tied it there myself. I pulled and jerked at it with the last of my strength but it was fast.

I thought as clearly as my battered head would allow me to think. I was in some danger, I was very weak, the skin on my arms and legs was raw, I doubted whether I was strong enough to climb out of the chair again. I looked up towards the horizon and saw a ship steaming past *Iskra* quite close. I saw no one on deck, no sign that I had been seen. Just as well, I thought, there wasn't much they could do for me. I had got myself into this predicament, there was no one to get me out of it. If I climbed out of the chair and slid down the mast or the shrouds I would leave all my halyards behind, leave myself no means of hoisting sail or of climbing the mast again without great difficulty. I can climb the mast without a chair but not a mast swinging through an arc of twenty feet every three seconds. Why not shift the chair from the throat to the peak halyard which was still free, attaching a line to the block so that I could pull it down when I got to the deck?

I cut *Iskra*'s flag halyard which was there beside me and tied it to the block, then I started to change the chair to the peak halyard block, pulling up the slack to take the weight, raising myself a few inches, enough to free the chair from the throat halyard and hook on the peak. Now at last I was clear of this mad tangle - all I had to do was lower away. Then *Iskra* ran into the wash of the ship. I could see the rolling waves from my perch aloft. Suddenly all was confusion and turmoil. The mast began to whip from side to side with extraordinary force; I was swung twenty or thirty feet back and forth every few seconds when she rolled and pitched. My hands were torn free of the mast, shrouds, halyards, my head crashed against the mast. I lost consciousness.

When I woke up I was hanging upside down by my feet which were caught round the ropes of the bo'sun's chair. I remember looking down at the sky, at the top of *Iskra*'s mast, seeing the horizon below me as she rolled and as I swung from side to side, showing a clear line of sea which swung in and out of my view. I thought, 'This is the end - I shall never get out of this; if I can free my feet I shall drop on my head on the deck or drop overboard, *Iskra* steaming slowly away from me.' Then my hands, stretched out over my head, downwards, came against *Iskra*'s starboard shrouds. Instinctively I gripped them - one in one hand and one in the other. I twisted my feet first one way and then the other and then both of them came free of the chair. I swung through 180 degrees in a perfect arc like a circus clown on a trapeze and my feet came to rest exactly on *Iskra*'s side light screens. I found myself standing there, quite overcome with astonishment, looking down at the deck no more than six feet below me. I said, 'I'm alive, I'm alive, I'm alive, I'm alive.' I jumped down to the deck, almost falling when the weight came on my legs, went into the cabin, opened the drink locker and poured myself a dram of brandy, repeating out loud, 'I'm alive, I'm alive, I'm alive - Wendy, I'm alive'. I was pleased to be alive.

The ordeal was not quite over. I seemed to be making my way through Purgatory, but slowly. If I could keep going until it ended I must be admitted to the gates. America could not be a land of damp gales and grey discomfort. It was a question of going on, desperately slowly but always on; and in the end I must come through to the other side of this Gulf Stream.

I cleared away the fall of the throat halyard, pulled on the cut flag halyard and the chair, with all its bits and pieces still attached to it, came sliding down. I fixed the block back on the gaff with a spare wire strop I had in the bo'sun's locker. A breeze came up from the south-west and soon *Iskra* was pushing into it in the same old way. I slept like a dead man for six hours, oblivious of the steadily rising wind, the lowering sky, the falling barometer; my automatic waking mechanism superseded by an exhaustion of such depth that I would not have been roused even if *Iskra* had turned herself upside down. I woke suddenly in the night when a heavy sea fell on the coach roof. She was plunging and rearing again with too much sail on her, the wind setting up its familiar, depressing whine through the rigging. 'Rising wind and falling glass,' I muttered. 'Soundly sleeps a careless ass.'

One look was enough - the mainsail would have to come off. I rolled up the jib, put on my harness and blundered for'ard, still half asleep, my actions governed by instinct, not proper thought. I let go the halyards again and clawed down the sail. The throat came down, the peak was reluctant. I cursed silently. I'd forgotten to let loose the lee runner, the sail was pressed against it. I ran to the cockpit, let go the runner and pulled on the leech of the sail, something I would never have done in my right mind. The heavy gaff came crashing down with a run. There was daylight enough for me to see the end of the halyard go snaking off up the mast, pass through the block at the top and drop down to the deck. 'Oh my God.' The tears poured out of me. I set the storm trysail and settled *Iskra* on course, weeping like a child and crying out in despair. I would have to go up the mast again before the wounds had healed from my last ascent.

The gale wore through its pattern; hard from the south-west for a day, then veering north-west and slowly easing, then a calm.

I spent the day and the night in a state of deep misery, feeling my lacerated arms and legs, trying to work out in my mind how I was going to climb that mast again. The scrapes were still painful, not serious but still stinging and making me wince when they came against something solid. Perhaps I could finish the voyage with the storm trysail? There was no more than 250 miles to go by my reckoning, I could already hear, faintly, three RDF stations on the coast - Great Duck, Monanan and Chatham. But I knew I couldn't do it. Anyway, my Dolphin would have none of it. This was no way to arrive in a new country, limping in under a jury rig because I was too inept to climb the mast. 'Just get on and do it,' he said.

This time I used my head. I put on the heaviest pair of trousers I had, a thick shirt with long sleeves, shoes and socks. I hooked the chair to the throat halyard again. This time I didn't shackle it to a shroud; and this time I left the storm trysail set and this time I dropped the fall of the halyard overboard with a winch handle fast to it so that it would sink into the sea as I hauled myself up. It wouldn't foul this time unless a whale took it. This time it was easy. When I swung with *Iskra*'s roll I fell harmlessly into the soft folds of the trysail. If my leg came against the stays, even with the old sores, I hardly felt it through the trousers. I climbed quickly to the crosstrees with the end of the halyard tied to the chair, reached up and threaded it through the block. Then I let myself down and as I came, the fall of the throat halyard came up out of the sea. When I got back to the deck I was laughing and shaking with fright all at the same time. A breeze came up from the north-east. I set my beautiful mainsail again and soon *Iskra* was bowling south with a brisk fair wind, everything set and keenly driving her on, right up to her big white topsail.

I was through Purgatory - everything was different. The sky came blue, the sea a pale aquamarine, cold and exhilarating after the tepid, sultry sludge of the Stream. Gulls wheeled round *Iskra*'s wake, my Dolphin's kith and kin leapt and cavorted all round him, twisting and interweaving their lithe bodies one with another and leaping out of the sea in a dance of delight as if to welcome him to this new continent. I did all my washing, washed myself, dried all my clothes, tidied and cleaned *Iskra*'s cabin, ate a huge meal with the last of my fresh vegetables and sang at the top of my voice, all depression left behind with the depressions of the Stream. I had been thirty-two days at sea and *Iskra* had come right through the westerlies, straight as an arrow, albeit an arrow with a few twists and turns in it. Now she was pointing for the Nantucket light with a spanking fair wind behind her.

I forgot the travails and traumas of the voyage; they were all in the past, behind me, folded into the album of unfathomable memory to be brought out and turned over in the mind, inspected, savoured, in some future reverie. Wendy would arrive in a few days, *Iskra* would be there to meet her; our romance would nourish itself with all the trials of our separation serving only to strengthen it, tighten the knot that held us together so that no hand could ever untie it. The day was perfect, the evening a mantle of glory to cover its perfection, the sun falling into the ocean ahead with a golden splendour, the moon hoisting its round squashy face out of the ocean astern. In the night the wind slowly died, leaving *Iskra* at peace on a calm sea, the confusion and rolling and crashing of the gear dissolved into the past.

The next day was fine and calm. I dived overboard for a swim, receiving a shock from the cold Labrador current. I still had 150 miles to go, I still had to fetch round Nantucket Island, and weather the extensive shoals to the southwest of it in order to reach Newport. I saw from my chart that there was a shoal water passage between the island and Cape Cod but without local knowledge and a local tide table I would never attempt it. A faint breeze came up from the south-west, the prevailing wind on this coast and *Iskra* was taken slowly towards Cape Cod. My position from sights was confirmed by a radio bearing of Chatham. It was still going to be a long beat in a light head wind and against the current before I could ease away for Newport. Soon I saw land. It was a long, low line of sand, all wreathed in haze, shimmering in the morning sun. It was the same landfall the Pilgrim Fathers made in 1620. They went round the east of the Cape with a fair wind and founded Provincetown.

I saw a small boat at anchor about half a mile distant under *Iskra*'s lee bow. As we ghosted closer I saw that she was a fishing boat, about sixteen feet long with a cuddy over her bow, *Red Rose* across her stern, a man fishing with lines. As I got closer I saw him haul a codfish. He was perhaps middle-aged, with a long peaked cap - a cod fisherman off Cape Cod. This was tradition; I felt as if *Iskra* might be the *Spray* and me a rogue reincarnation of Captain Slocum. I saw him bait his line and cast it again as *Iskra* drew closer. He looked at her with an appraising eye, a seaman's eye; I saw him scrutinize her rig, her ensign, her bowsprit, the cut of her sails, I saw him gaze at my Dolphin. I said, 'Good Morning'. There was a pause for a moment and then he said 'Hi'. There was another pause. *Iskra* was within a few feet of him. I saw him jogging his line. The *Red Rose* was rocking gently in the swell. *Iskra* was almost becalmed, stemming a weak current. 'Where'r ya from?' he asked. 'England.' 'Is that so?' There was a pause again. The conversation seemed to have reached its logical end. I could think of nothing more to say. He seemed to be weighing the news in his mind, turning it over, considering it. I had heard that New Englanders are slow to reach their judgements, reluctant to jump to quick conclusions. Then he said, 'Welcome to America'.

XI

America

Ed Tucker took a line and tied *Iskra* alongside the *Red Rose*. He gave me the codfish he had just caught. He came on board and looked round the cabin. He knew about boats, knew about English designers like Maurice Griffiths and David Hillyard, had read about the schooner *Integrity*. He told me it had been one of his life's ambitions to make an ocean passage in a small boat. When I gave him a copy of my *Integrity* book out of *Iskra*'s fo'c'sle locker he was my friend for life. He talked to the coastguard on his VHF and then towed *Iskra* close in to the beach where I dropped the anchor. He went off in the *Red Rose*, taking Wendy's telephone number with him and saying he would be back soon.

It was a flat calm. I decided to wait for Ed to come back before going off. We had looked at the chart together and decided it would be dangerous for me to go through the Pollock Rip channel between the Cape and Nantucket Island. The place is a devil's cauldron of shoals with a fierce tide sweeping across them and channels between which, Ed told me, shift their position with every gale. My English chart was small scale and quite inadequate. In this light weather it would take me at least two days to sail the 150 miles round the Nantucket Shoal. I wanted to be sure that Wendy knew that I had arrived and I decided to wait for Ed to come back. I could see from the chart that he would be some time; it was a fair distance through the Monomoy Passage to Chatham.

I had half arrived. I could see it, smell it, even hear it but still not be there. Immigration laws are strict. The coast guard told Ed on the VHF that it would not be possible for me to land at Chatham, which is not an entry port to the United States. In any case, it would be hard to get *Iskra* in to Chatham. Ed could manage comfortably in the *Red Rose* but it was a shallow sandy place like all the coast on the outside of the Cape. As there was no wind anyway I contented myself to wait. It was a pleasant change to be at anchor and *Iskra* still again, even if the voyage was not yet over.

Ed came back in the evening laden with gifts and good news. He brought me the daily paper and a selection of gifts hurriedly thrown together by his wife - four cans of beer, a fresh lemon, a

CAPE COD

chatham

shoals

NANTUCKET
SOUND

Pollock Rip
channel

shoals

Tuckernuck
Island

NANTUCKET

loaf of bread, two tins of tomato juice, a hamburger and, lastly, a copy of Eldridge's tide tables showing the set and strength of the current and all the depths in the Pollock Rip channel. The good news was of Wendy. Ed had spoken to her on the telephone - she was well, she sent me her love, she was coming in five days. Ed had paid for the call, Wendy told me afterwards, refusing to reverse the charges as I had made him promise to do. My first encounter with an American in America set the pattern for the rest of the voyage. With few exceptions everyone loved us and we loved everyone. When I looked at my Dolphin his expression had relaxed its tough, obstinate look. 'Don't be previous,' I said to him, 'we're not there yet.'

I ate my way through Ed's codfish, flavoured with fresh lemon, fresh potatoes and onions, and fresh bread washed down with beer and while I ate I perused Eldridge's tide tables. They gave me a map of the channel for each hour of the tide. It would be high water at nine in the morning; the ebb runs in through the channel instead of out as a stranger might expect and would be fair for me. It was a twisting, ferocious looking place but it was well marked and in calm weather with good visibility I should be able to get through it. I could see the first of the buoys close to where *Iskra* was anchored. It would save me the best part of 100 miles. 'Don't use it if there's fog,' Ed had warned, 'you'll get lost.' Once through it I would be in sheltered water in the Nantucket Sound and the Vineyard Sound, leaving only a short fifteen miles of open sea across to Newport. Ed had pointed out to me a good refuge in Tarpaulin Cove where I would be able to spend the night. The wind when it came, he predicted, would be from the south-east which would allow me to fetch. I slept all night full of food and drink and happy thoughts.

The morning was calm again and clear. I looked at it, sniffed the still air. 'I'll risk it,' I thought; 'if I go round it might take three days.' I ate my breakfast, hoisted the mainsail; even though there was no wind it would be better to be ready for the breeze when it came. Then I started to haul in the chain. I had let go thirty fathoms - it was hard work. I worked slowly, stopping every five minutes to go below and stow the locker as I hauled the chain in. *Iskra* anchors with chain, not rope. With chain I can use a smaller anchor which I can handle myself more easily. When she was over it I started the engine and left it idling, then I broke the anchor out, hauled it on deck, stowed it and lashed it down. When I looked up from my work there was a thick fog.

I couldn't see even the first of the buoys which I knew was no more than 200 yards away. Well, that settled it, there would be no Pollock Rip channel for me, I would make my way round the outside. If it took a long time, well, the voyage had taken a long time. I set course for the first buoy, I had marked its bearing in the log. I would use it as a point of departure, then steer offshore until I was well clear of the land and set course parallel to the coast. I soon picked it up. I heard it first, a low, sonorous whistle and soon it materialised out of the fog, close alongside, a great black fellow that looked like the front part of a Rocky Mountains steam engine. There was still an hour before high water, the current was nearly slack, perhaps I could wait for a little while, perhaps the fog would clear. I stopped the engine, allowing *Iskra* to drift.

Rivers of moisture ran down her sails and gathered in fat drops along the bottom of the boom. The fog swirled round the mast, cocooning *Iskra* in a tight ball of grey wool. The deep sad note of the buoy came out of the thickness like funeral music echoing round the spaces of a cathedral. Then in the silence between the whistles I heard the sound of a bell. At first it didn't occur to me what it was, a sound from the shore perhaps, or from a ship at anchor. Then I realised - what an idiot. I looked at the chart, the next buoy was a bell. Why not go for it? This was easy. I could listen my way through the Pollock Rip from whistle to bell, bell to whistle.

I took a bearing of the direction of the bell, started the engine and set course for it. I couldn't hear it with the engine running so I stopped the engine after ten minutes and listened again. At first I could hear nothing. *Iskra* lay shrouded in the fog in silence, only the plop of the drops falling from the boom and the indefinable, hushed rustle that is the noise the ocean makes in a calm. Then the bell rang out, close astern. I had passed it. The sea was so calm that the buoy was still, with no movement to operate the bell except an occasional undulation in the swell.

I listened for a few minutes and then I heard the next whistle, over to port. Yes, that was right from the chart. I set course and started the engine; stopped it in six minutes and heard the whistle ahead and close. This was easy. I came close up to the buoy until it loomed out of the fog, so close that *Iskra* nearly hit it. I marked its number 3 on the chart. Now the sea was lumpy, the little brown waves slapping against *Iskra*'s side. Already the tide had her in its grip and was running fast. I saw it streaming against the buoy as it glided silently past. Now she was pitching in short jerks and the engine seemed to be giving her little way. I set course for the next bell.

Then wind came - from right ahead. The mainsail began to shake. The waves increased in size suddenly, bringing *Iskra* to a halt so that I was hardly able to keep her head to wind. I would have to sail - stop the engine and tack from side to side of the narrow, twisting channel. There could be no turning back against this current. It was already rough. It was hard to see how fast she was going. After ten minutes I put her about. In another ten minutes I put her about again. I could hear nothing, no bell, no whistle. The buoy ought to be close aboard now. The channel made a dog-leg here, through the shallowest part, first to starboard for half a mile and then to port. *Iskra*'s echo sounder wasn't working - it hadn't been used since leaving England, now it had given up. 'Christ - it looks shallow.' I found the lead line in a cockpit locker, swung it on the lee side and let it go. It plopped into the water, hit the bottom at once. One and a half fathoms. *Iskra* draws five feet. 'If she hits this sand she will break to pieces'.

I tried to think clearly. I was sweating, shaking all over. I keep a packet of glucose tablets in the chart drawer and I crunched two of them, feeling the sugar flow into the blood stream, calming the nerves, giving concentration, strength. I was lost. The fog was as thick as ever - I would have expected the wind to blow it away but it didn't. I might have passed the buoy, I might be to one side of it. The wind was freshening - this would make it harder to hear the buoys. She would have to be reefed, water was beginning to break aboard. It was urgent, she had to be reefed regardless of anything else. I left her on the port tack. If she was beyond the buoy she would go over one shoal, if she was before it she would go over another. Both of them dried four feet at low water; it wasn't an hour after high water - she ought to go over them. Eldridge said the rise of the tide was ten feet. It was with the gods.

I clipped on my harness, went for'ard and lowered the halyards. From the foredeck I could see the cockpit through the fog, the tide rip leaping all around. I could see my Dolphin below the bowsprit, all washed by the sea. 'You get us out - you've got brains, instinct, cunning, knowledge. Get us out.' I worked as quickly as I knew how, expecting every moment to feel the bottom on her keel. The sea was brown with suspended sand, like the Thames estuary. In ten minutes she was easier. I threw the lead over again. One fathom. I put her about. Now I didn't know where the tide had taken her - she might be anywhere. I knew if she hit the sand in this sea she would be broken - what an end to the voyage. 'Get us out of it Dolphin.' I shouted.

Then I heard a whistle far away, over to starboard. I jumped down to the chart table. It wasn't a bell, it was a whistle. It must be the one after the bell. It was to starboard - how far? There was a shoal beside it, between us and it. We were in shallow water but it was shallower between *Iskra* and the buoy. We would have to keep on. I threw the lead again nine feet. We'd keep on for a mile, then come round on the other tack.

In ten minutes it shallowed again, down to six feet - even less perhaps. I put her about. She came flapping and shaking into the wind. I thought I felt her touch, a faint jar, the lightest bump. Oh Christ. She filled on the other tack, heeled over and raced off. Now I could hear nothing - no bell, no whistle. The lead refused to go further down than the one fathom mark. The chart was a conundrum; it was small scale, showing the whole of the Cape and Nantucket Island; the numbers of the buoys were not shown. The tidal map in Eldridge was a better guide but I was lost. I was bemused by the fog; with this fierce tide, the tacking every few minutes and the sounding with the lead I had kept no record of courses and changes of direction and times. I was exhausted by the tension. 'If there's fog you'll get lost I guess.' Ed had said.

Then the sounding slowly increased. From the one fathom mark they gained imperceptibly, inch by inch. One and a half fathoms was safe, two fathoms was luxury. The wind backed a point, allowing *Iskra* to fetch the course down the sound from whatever point of the bank we had come through. The fog grew thinner, a watery sun peered through the cover of cloud. As the visibility improved I saw a low line of coast far away to port - Nantucket Island no doubt. Soundings increased until I no longer cast the lead. A buoy appeared ahead and slightly to port, by hauling the sheets I could fetch it. It was a brother to the one I had seen early in the day. It was number 17. We were clear. 'Thank you Dolphin.' I said, 'Thank you.'

Now it was a wonderful sail, in a strong wind through the sheltered sound, *Iskra* showing me that she had not forgotten how to sail fast, my Dolphin wearing his old, confident, carefree smile. Soon I began to see other yachts, the first I had seen at sea since leaving Dartmouth; they waved cheerily when they saw the red ensign and the yellow quarantine flag flying from the crosstrees. Soon the shores of Nantucket Island closed and I picked up the Elizabeth Islands on the east side of the sound and passed Martha's Vineyard.

Whatever the discomforts and harassments of the sea, the worst it can do to frighten, to exhaust, to batter with wind and wet and cold, to discourage with contrary winds and foul currents and perilous shallows, a few hour's brisk fair wind on a bright day puts them all out of mind. The sea has this facility to clear the slate, to wipe away in a few hours a month of distress. When the ocean smiles, its all-embracing good humour sends the malevolence packing. The essential optimism which is a part of all people who follow the sea in small boats is rekindled every time the sun shines and the breeze blows fair. I anchored in Tarpaulin Cove among a dozen yachts, proud of *Iskra* and proud of my Dolphin. I slept the night with the remains of Ed Tucker's cod and his last two cans of beer inside me. Next day I sailed across to Newport, dropped the anchor in its spacious harbour and wrote 'End of Passage' in the log.

One of the differences in attitudes between Americans and the English, I found to my advantage, concerns books and writers. In England the profession of writing is a humble one; books are rated low, writers are expected to be, and are, poor. Unless a writer is lucky enough to find a publisher who will work with him, helping him to produce copy which is good and at the same time saleable, he may find himself at odds with his bread and butter. Amateurs with little knowledge and less sensibility, posing as publishers' editors, will hack his manuscripts to pieces, without consulting the author, and then offer them to the public as his work. To protest, consigns a writer to a blacklist as an awkward customer, so that he is unlikely to get his work accepted or even looked at again. I have usually found that publishers have failed to sell the print run of my books, remaindering them to save the storage cost. I have always bought this remainder, which under the contract must be offered to me first and have sold them off myself at the full price, thus making for myself a useful profit. As a salesman, armed with the rejected plunder of my own work, I have touted them round from shop to shop, selling them in twos and threes and sometimes tens until they are all gone. They have always been bought by the public at the marked price, as much in spite of as because of publishers. I have made more money from selling my books to shops and direct to the public than I have ever made from royalties, and I have had the additional bonus of making friends in many parts of the world among people who have bought my books from me. I offer a money-back guarantee with each book. 'If you don't enjoy it, bring it back and I'll refund you the money.' I say. So far I have not lost by this stratagem.

The first people I met on the American continent, after Ed Tucker, were a couple whose boat was moored near where *Iskra* dropped anchor. They were enchanted when they heard I was a writer, asked if I had any of my books and bought them from me at once. They came on board to welcome me as soon as I arrived in Newport harbour, took me ashore with their outboard motor and came with me when I went to clear Customs and Immigration, formalities which were completed in minutes. I was pleased to have them with me because I found I could hardly walk when I first went ashore. The land reeled under my feet, I tripped over a stone as I staggered across the dock and fell headlong, grazing my leg badly.

The next day I took my books to all the bookshops in Newport, including Ron Barr's Armchair Sailor, probably the best nautical bookshop anywhere. The book buyers were all pleased to buy my books and treated me with an informal friendly courtesy which I often found in America and which is a rarity in similar circumstances in England. In America both writers and salesmen are respected - even revered. My books provided me with a steady income for all the time I was in America and Canada. Later, when Wendy came out, we sailed to Mystic Seaport in Long Island Sound where *Iskra* was an honoured guest. A small notice hung in the rigging was enough to bring a stream of people on board in search of books and they were put on sale in the seaport bookshop. I had a label printed which read, 'This book is one of 400 shipped to America on board the author's yacht *Iskra* in 1980. *Iskra* is a ten-ton gaff cutter built in Littlehampton, England. This single-handed voyage, her seventh across the Atlantic Ocean, is in celebration of her 50th birthday.' I stuck it on the title page of each book that came across the ocean with me.

From Mystic, Wendy and I sailed back to Buzzards Bay where we visited Waldo Howland in South Dartmouth and saw the boat shed in Padeneram where the *Integrity* was built. Everywhere we went we sold books. In the end I sold the American rights of *Schooner Integrity* and it was published in the USA in hardback and in paperback. All the books I brought to America were unharmed by the Gulf Stream and the Atlantic except a few copies of *Rustler on the Beach* which were stained with salt water from *Iskra*'s bilges. I sold them at a premium.

After our first cruise in America Wendy and I came back to England, leaving *Iskra* laid up in Providence, Rhode Island, in a friendly and inexpensive yard recommended to us by Hopie, who I had first met in Antigua, and her husband Bobby Goddard. I said farewell to my Dolphin and left *Iskra* afloat, lying on a strong mooring off the yard, all covered up with an old tarpaulin and protected by her copper sheathing. Her gear was neatly stowed away in a corner under the roof of Nunk Allen's boatshed. A friendly neighbour in the yard showed me how to 'winterize' the engine, the lavatory and all the pumps on board and I left her to her fate for the icy American winter. The temperature went down beyond minus twenty degrees Centigrade, the winter gales roared round her, even a spent hurricane swept up the east coast of America. Somehow she hung on grimly through the winter. Nunk Allen moved her from the mooring to alongside one of his docks so that he could more easily break the ice which built up round her. My friends in the yard adopted her as their personal responsibility, fussing over her, keeping her pumped dry and occasionally writing me reassuring notes about her condition. Hopie photographed her in the ice and snow, all stripped of her gear and spars. I spent a miserable winter in England worrying about her, wondering whether I would ever be able to go back and fetch her home.

My business was beginning to suffer grievously from escalating costs and reduced turnover. For a time it looked as if it would fold into the ground and leave me penniless, unable to meet my responsibilities. I had the dollars from books, which I had salted down in an American bank so that, come what may to the business, I would have the means to go back to my Dolphin, fit out my boat and provision her for her return across the ocean.

I did go back to America, leaving the business in a state no business should be left in, with insufficient working funds and falling receipts at a time when businesses were crumbling all over the City of London. *Iskra* was more important - she is irreplaceable, whereas a business can always be pulled together, or re-started if necessary. No one's money was involved except my own. *Iskra* had to be looked after and brought back to England; my Dolphin belongs in the sailmaker's yard in Maldon, Essex. I went off on the aeroplane in the early summer, my luggage loaded with more books to replenish *Iskra*'s stock. I went first to the west coast to give a slide lecture at the San Francisco Yacht Club, invited by a lady I had met in the Bahamas two years previously. They paid me what I considered an enormous sum of money and many books changed hands.

Iskra was a forlorn sight when I arrived in the silence of night at the yard in Providence, with an assortment of bags and packets and cardboard boxes and bundles, dumped at the yard gate from a taxi. I saw her at once. She had been moved out to her mooring again; I could see her in the faint moonlight, a gaunt shape all cocooned in tarpaulin like a water slug, her mast protruding up into the night, casting a rippled shadow across the calm water. It was cold, drizzling. I found a dinghy, loaded my gear and sculled on board. It seemed an unlikely conceit that this vessel could carry me back over all those miles of ocean I had just crossed so swiftly in an aeroplane.

As I got near her I heard the old familiar whisper of water round her hull. It was her welcome back for me. I lifted the cover and climbed into the cockpit. She was unlocked, as always. I slid the hatch and went below. I struck a match, lit an oil lamp, the shades and shadows jumped out at me. She was the same - my place. The varnished chart table glistened in the soft light, the port-holes gazed at me with wise eyes, the oil painting of my old house threw back its familiarity, the coins in a line fixed to the bulkhead, one for every country she has visited, from Norway to Cuba, the kettle poking up his spout from the galley stove, the little picture Wendy gave me when I left England, five crossed kisses on the back, the book cases with my precious volumes, brass chart dividers, the hand bearing compass. She was dry and warm and she smelled of boat and sanity and happiness. My Dolphin was propped up on the fo'c'sle bunk, taken off his perch under the bowsprit against the winter storms. He was grinning again, right across his chubby countenance.

I spent two weeks fitting out and then set off for Boston where Wendy would come on an aeroplane. First I made a round of the book shops, replenishing their stocks. The yard in Providence was a friendly, efficient and not expensive establishment run by Nunk Allen and his sons and daughter. My bill was offset by the sale of books in the yard chandlery. *Iskra*'s fit-out was perfunctory, she was beginning to show signs of her long, rough journey. She was slipped and her copper bottom cleaned and scrubbed and painted, her gear overhauled, the old diesel roused into life, the Dolphin restored to his place under the bowsprit. On a fine day with a friend on board we sailed down Narragansett Bay to Newport to be entertained by Hope until the time came to leave for Boston. I forgot about business, its very existence went out of my mind. The hurly-burly of getting *Iskra* ready for her long cruise up the east coast of America, through Maine to Nova Scotia, perhaps even to Newfoundland before setting off for home, was enough to drive every mundane thought away.

Sailing boats are like that - they fill all the regions of the mind with their own urgent needs and problems, excluding all else. They instil a naive optimism so that nothing seems impossible. Wendy would come for a month, we would cruise for a thousand miles and then I would sail back, taking a long loop to the south perhaps and calling in at Horta in the Azores on my way home. I was to meet her in Boston and after a weekend together she was to fly to Los Angeles to a conference she was attending. Meanwhile I would take *Iskra* up to Portland, Maine where she would join me again when the conference was over and the cruise would begin. It all seemed easy. When I got back to England I would lay *Iskra* up in her mud berth at Maldon and then it would be time enough to see about business.

Iskra was in Boston with a day in hand for me to see the new publisher of *Schooner Integrity* which was to be re-titled, *The Death of the Schooner Integrity* for the American edition and to spread my books around the city. I waited at the airport for Wendy's plane to arrive, watched from a glass terrace as it glided in to land, saw the passengers spill to the ground like eggs from a broody hen, stood waiting an age as she hatched out from the Customs shed and hurried her on board *Iskra*. Her brief luggage was loaded into *Iskra*'s rubber dinghy and rowed out to a borrowed mooring off Lewis Wharf. I had her at last, for a whole weekend. We seem to spend our lives meeting and departing from trains, airports, bus stations.

Boston is the nicest city I know; for that weekend it was converted to Heaven. At dawn the skyscrapers sway together in the mist like reeds in a pond. The city has an air of suppressed excitement as if it would suddenly burst into song or dance or some purposeless violence. In the flea market buskers sing and play to huge audiences, men free themselves from padlocked chains, magicians perform incredible tricks. We walked among the glass mountains, gazing up at the mirrored towers, through parks and gardens by the Charles River, threaded the maze of the Italian quarter, ate spaghetti, drank Californian wine and tottered back to *Iskra* in the night to find ourselves in a private world within a world, a piece of home amidst the fantasy which breathes through every American city. Boats are like that as well. They furnish a context, allow the impressions and mental pictures to be fitted together into a continuous whole. *Iskra* is home wherever we go. When people visit her, as we visited homes in America, they come to know us through our home just as we know them through theirs.

The day Wendy went off to Los Angeles the fog came down thick and heavy. It persisted through the day and the next day and the next so that I lost all sight of the city from my mooring off Lewis Wharf. I asked people I knew 'How long will it last?' 'Who knows? Maybe a week, maybe another day, maybe an hour. You'll just have to wait I guess.' On the third day I could wait no longer. I had no telephone number for Wendy in Los Angeles, no way of telling her I might not be in Portland when she arrived. I slipped the mooring early in the morning, hoisted the mainsail into this dank, opaque air and sailed from buoy to buoy. Jet aeroplanes from Boston's international airport roared invisibly through the fog as we sailed out of the harbour. Ferries, with their radar, skirted round us, hooting mournfully. I listened intently for the alternate bells and whistles which I had learned about in the Pollock Rip channel. I kept to the side of the channel, feeling my way from one mark to the next, hearing the ships' engines and sometimes the swish of their bow waves as they passed me. I skirted Deer Island without seeing it, no more than a few yards off. What breeze there was came from ahead. I made a leg out to seaward, hoping that by the time I closed the land again on the inshore tack the fog would lift. It didn't. I could see nothing as I approached the shore in the afternoon, standing on towards the cliffs to the west of Gloucester until I could hear the shore - motor cars, music from some enterprise, its undulating sound carried out through the fog, even the echo of *Iskra*'s fog horn thrown back from the cliff face. The wind eased to nothing.

I started the engine and steered parallel to the coast. If I went on for long enough I must hear the fog horn on the pier head at the entrance to Gloucester harbour. Every half an hour I stopped the engine and listened. I was tired; steering all day to keep *Iskra* steady on course for fear of losing myself, listening, worrying. Wendy would be in Portland the day after next. By evening, I had covered the distance according to my reckoning. I stopped the engine and listened again. I heard it ahead - a sad sonorous call of welcome and relief. In half an hour I was close to it. Now it filled the whole world with its resonance; I could hear its deep breath, like a snoring giant. *Iskra* passed within feet of the harbour wall, the sound bellowing at me from above, until it died out astern as I entered the harbour and headed cautiously for the yacht anchorage marked on my chart. A yacht at her mooring loomed through the fog - the first object I had seen since leaving Boston. I passed close to her, where there was one mooring there would be others. I saw one ahead, grabbed it with the boat hook and made it fast.

The next morning the fog was as thick but there was a breeze. *Iskra* left Gloucester at dawn, without seeing a stick of it, sailing past the same fog horn and heading for Cape Anne. If there had been no fog I would have taken her through the canal that runs from Gloucester through to the other side of the Cape, cutting off half a day's sail. Now it was rough, with a strong head wind, but the fog refused to be blown away. It flowed past like dense smoke from a bonfire, cutting out the visual world; all I could see were waves breaking across the foredeck, grey seas within a tight circle and the sail reaching up into grey emptiness.

Fog plays tricks on a tired man alone. I listened for those low whistles, willing the sound to come, imagining it before its time. When I did hear it the sound would dance about, changing its direction so convincingly that I would alter *Iskra* a point, or two points, although I knew by all the logic of my navigation that the buoy could not be there. Sometimes the sound would seem close, only a few boat's lengths away and then it would fade to the far distance. I would have to stop listening, go below and consciously relax for a moment with a book or a cup of tea so that the sound could fall back to its proper bearing and distance. To reassure myself I took *Iskra* right up close to the buoy off Boon Island to read its number and be certain.

The night brought a denser blackness, an eerie isolation. We were outside all reality, suspended in some empty wilderness of black nothing where there was no direction, no time, no balance. We were like spacemen, gliding through an empty universe bound from nowhere to nowhere. *Iskra's* cabin seemed unfamiliar. I saw the things I knew as if for the first time, the almanac, the hand bearing compass, the clock, the barometer - all were new to me. I tried to sleep as *Iskra* lay becalmed but the fog was oppressive; my mind raced and whirled, encompassing every kind of disaster. I had to start the engine to bring in a fixed reality, its steady thump, the necessity of steering, brought me back to the real world. In the morning I picked up the RDF signal from the buoy off Portland and motored towards it, keeping the course until I saw its huge platform shape immediately in front of *Iskra's* bowsprit. I was in harbour at eleven. Wendy arrived at one.

Maine destroyed my finely calculated plans for *Iskra's* return to England. It was paradise. The notion that Wendy and I could hurry through it leaving its delights behind us within a week, which we would have to do if I was to continue the voyage as I had intended, soon became ridiculous. We were on a kind of honeymoon; the myriad islands of Maine, the emptiness of it, the beaches, the dark woods, the blue skies and deep cold sea, clams, mussels, oysters for the taking, the soft fair breezes were more temptation than we had will to withstand. We meandered from place to place soaking in the charm of 'down east' Maine. We met people from other boats and from ashore who entertained us and we them. We sold books all the way up the coast, enough to line our larder until they were all gone. The further east we went the more we were removed from civilisation. Maine has a quality of remote grandeur, an aloof dignity as if it was the last place left where peace and tranquility hold sway, despising with a haughty disdain the commercial bustle of the Massachusetts coast.

Iskra wound her way in and around the islands regardless of time, regardless of worldly worries, right up to Grand Manan Island, the Canadian border and the Bay of Fundy. We anchored in Musquash harbour, surrounded by the limitless spaces of the

Canadian forest lands. The people we met in this remoteness had never seen an English yacht. We passed through Saint John, New Brunswick, where we sold the last of the books and penetrated the reversing falls into the rural seclusion of the Saint John river, a stretch of wooded, rolling farmland, empty, quiet, eminently at peace. The falls are a phenomenon of the fifty foot tides of the Bay of Fundy. At full flood and full ebb the difference in the levels of river and bay causes a ten foot waterfall as the two masses of water meet in a narrow gorge at the entrance to the river. For a quarter of an hour at the change of the tide *Iskra* could pass through a swirling, restless calm. At all other times it would be destruction.

In the Saint John river the honeymoon ended - Wendy had to go back. We telephoned England, the thin wire connecting us to reality again. 'If you don't come back now, you won't have a business to come back to.' It was a stunning shock. For two months I had given no thought to reality. *Iskra* would have to stay in America for another winter. It was urgent for me to fly back at once or we would be broke.

On our way through Maine we had been told about Tom and Toot by a friend. 'If you're thinking of staying another winter,' he had said, 'you could try Tom and Toot in Sorrento, they might haul you out. They're not 'yachty', mind you - you'd have to do

Toot

161

all your own work of course.' The yards in the Saint John river were expensive and the air fare from Canada back to England was nearly twice as expensive as from Boston. The yards in the yachting resorts of Maine were also expensive, out of our class with their smart chandleries, white painted sheds, offices and pretty secretaries.

We took *Iskra* 200 miles back along the coast from Canada to Maine and sailed into East Point, Sorrento, dropped anchor off the beach in a bay enclosed by wooded islands and rowed ashore in our rubber dinghy. Tom and Toot were leaning against a lobster boat idly watching our arrival. 'Someone told us you might haul our boat out for the winter.' They looked at us with mild interest. Wendy, carrying her shoes, mud half-way up her legs, a blue sun hat confining her long, ginger hair, big round sunglasses, looked like a film star on location. Tom unwound himself to his full height, pushed back the peak of his hat and his face slowly split into a smile. 'Guess we might.' he said, looking out over the anchorage to where *Iskra* lay. 'Where'r ya from?' 'England.' 'How'd ya get here?' 'Sailed.' We were friends.

It was time for Wendy to go - her flight was booked. I sailed her the six miles to Bar Harbour, waved another goodbye and turned back for Sorrento, alone again. I never used to be lonely - this was a new experience. In my childhood I lived alone in a dream world of my own; I have always flourished by myself, now I don't like it. I sailed *Iskra* back to Sorrento with a sick feeling in my stomach.

The next day was Sunday and I saw no sign of activity on the shore. I busied myself with my part of the haul out. *Iskra*'s rig demands an array of cordage up the mast which must all be taken off in the winter - eight halyards including gear for the topsail and running sails for the trade winds. I stripped all this running rigging, took off the bowsprit and the steering vane, rubber dinghy, life-raft and all her sails, and carried them to the store where Tom had given me a place under the keel of another boat. My Dolphin was unscrewed from his place and cradled in a nest of ropes and wires on the fo'c'sle bunk, safe from the snow and gales of the Maine winter.

Toot liked the steering vane 'It steers all night?' he asked. He thought about this for a few moments. 'I guess it don't eat nothing,' he said. 'Good hand to have aboard I guess.' 'Yeah,' said Tom, 'It don't get no wages, don't get drunk in harbour,

162

don't go out with women 'n' things like that. Yeah, I guess that's a good hand to have aboard.'

A cradle had been conjured up from somewhere in the yard and dragged down to the low water mark. It was made of pine logs and sections of complete trees. The side runners were each substantial timbers, thirty-five feet long and nearly two feet in diameter, the cross pieces bolted through the runners and spiked with huge nails. *Iskra*'s keel would be supported by baulks of pine and she would sit in chocks made up of four-by-four-inch timber spiked to the cradle. The whole contraption would slide across the ground on runners. It was made to go both ways, forwards out of the sea and backwards into the sea next spring.

Two loads of rocks lay in piles on the shore to be placed along the runners so that the cradle would stay on the bottom when the tide came up and *Iskra* was floated into it - a simple and ingenious arrangement. I didn't understand where the motive power was to come from, except perhaps from a torpid rusty giant of a vehicle called 'The Incredible Hulk'. It had a small winch on the back with a coil of good wire, but it was a preposterous vehicle. The front was battered beyond recognition, the massive bumper was pulled out of shape, where there had been lights only jagged holes remained with an occasional loose wire as a reminder of the past. The seat was all springs, the speedometer was stuck nostalgically at 65, the gear lever had a piece of string attached to keep it in second, the floor of the cab was gone exposing the bowels of this monstrous machinery. In some way 'The Incredible Hulk', like Tom himself, had an air of sleeping power as if some fairy wand might bring it to life.

Tom said. 'Well, there's your cradle I guess; you can put her in on the tide this evening.' I loaded the cradle with the rocks and stones, then went aboard and started the engine for the last time, recovered the anchor and nosed in across the shallows to where I could see the sides of the cradle protruding above water. Tom left me hammer and nails, a few lengths of four-by-four and a pile of odd timber in the back of the truck and disappeared.

It was a quiet evening in Sorrento, East Point; the operation was taking on an unreal, even a sinister aspect. How could I do this on my own? Suppose they couldn't shift her? Or got her half-way up and could move her no further? Or the cradle collapsed, leaving her stranded on the shingle?

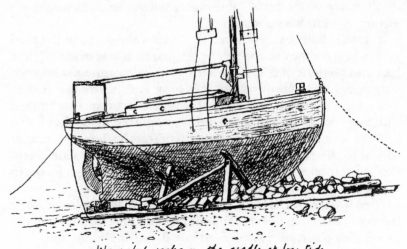

We piled rocks on the cradle at low tide

It was dark by the time the water left her. The trees and the sea and the beach looked black and foreboding - there was no sound, no light, no life. I started work with torches borrowed from Tom and Toot and chocked her up, fashioning the small stuff and wedging her so that she was solid and upright in the cradle. I took all the rocks and stones off the runners and threw them clear. I checked that the ground was free of obstructions in front of her. I finished at two o'clock in the morning. I fell into a kind of half-sleep in my bunk on board *Iskra*, puzzling in my mind how this operation was to be concluded, wondering whether I had chanced my boat in a senseless gamble to save a few dollars.

Early in the morning I heard a stirring from the lane towards the house, a kind of grinding, grating noise and then an uncertain cough followed by a splutter, a brief whirring and then silence. In a moment the cycle was repeated and then again, but now the splutter became a mature roar, the coughs a deep, throaty shudder and the whirring a full contralto whine. A thin column of smoke like an Indian signal ascended through the forest. The sound grew in stature until Tom arrived at the wheel of 'The Incredible Hulk' his face dark with concentration. He was in good time, before the morning tide had a chance to lift *Iskra* off the cradle. The great machine roared out its welcome to the new day. Instead of bringing the Hulk to the shore Tom drove it through the bushes and into a clearing at the top of a steep rise

164

above the beach. Then he turned it so that its back end was towards *Iskra*, far away, it seemed, across a patch of thick scrub and down the beach. 'Mornin', he said, 'guess you made a job of that cradle.'

With the air of a man pulling rabbits from a hat he produced a long heavy chain from the Hulk's back regions. Helped by Toot this was dragged into the forest and shackled round a tree. Then he released the clutch on the drum of wire and carried a bight down to *Iskra*, passing it through an iron swivel block on the cradle and back to the Hulk. 'Paid twelve dollars for two bits of chain like this' he said, 'best deal I ever made.' The act was beginning to look real. Clearly Tom knew more about hauling boats than I had given him credit for.

The Hulk roared into life, this time driving a shaft connected to the drum. A modest column of smoke rose into the air, the chain came taut, biting into the tree, the wire ran smooth through the snatch block, the bridle took the strain, *Iskra* began to move ahead. She came a few yards as smooth as butter until the water began to leave her and then Tom stopped the engine, pushed his hat back on his head and split into his grin. "I guess she'll come,' he said. I believe he knew the game was just beginning.

Now the beach sloped steeply, now *Iskra* no longer had the support of water round her hull. The whole weight of her would have to be pulled up a sharp incline. Tom slacked the wire off the drum again and rove it through two more blocks, so doubling the power of the tackle. Another chain was produced and fastened from another tree to the Hulk's front end, to stop it from sliding back. The noise rose to an all-embracing thunder, chains and wire bar tight and quivering with strain, smoke pouring, the Hulk itself shaking like an epileptic, one side of it lifting in the air as the chains came sickeningly taut. Tom balanced in the cab over the groaning, tortured machinery, his foot on the throttle, the gear lever held in place by the string and his knee jammed against it; *Iskra* moving slowly, painfully, up the slope.

Suddenly Toot yelled, 'Hey, stop ..... timber!' There was a tearing, crashing, rending sound, the very earth shook as the tree lifted out by the roots and fell gracefully with a crash and a shudder within a foot of 'The Incredible Hulk'. Then silence. The wire went slack, *Iskra* ceased to move. Tom emerged slowly, straightened his long form, stood beside the Hulk, pushed back his hat and said, 'I guess it'll take a year or two before we get another one like that.' His chin wore the rigid hard line of obstinacy.

More chain was found - another tree, bigger, stronger, further back; the Hulk's machinery roared again, blue smoke poured, *Iskra* inched forward. Tom's jaw set tighter, firmer; black smoke spewed, she moved a few feet then a noise like a hammer on a tin roof - a link of chain sprang apart and *Iskra* stopped again. But by now the fight was over. A new chain was found, one last convulsion from Hulk did it - black smoke and flames poured from the exhaust, the whole engine lifted off the ground by its own power, the chain bit into the big tree, *Iskra* slid over the ridge and settled herself for the winter beside an old houseboat on stilts, up out of sea and ice and all harm for the long months until I would come back.

My Dolphin found friends in Sorrento, Maine. Joe Greene fell in love with him, worried over *Iskra* through the winter, writing me long, soothing letters describing the fierce weather, the number of feet of snow, sending me the weather charts for the coast. He visited her often, tended the lashings of the old tarpaulin Tom had loaned me. Jim McCabe said, 'Don't worry - we'll keep our eye on her, I guess. Let me know when you come back and Lucy will meet you at the airport in Ellesmere. You'll stay with us until she's ready for you to live aboard again.' I patted her old grey sides and said goodbye to *Iskra* and to my Dolphin. I was leaving them among friends for another long winter.

Tom in the Incredible Hulk

XII

Home to Rest

I don't know how my Dolphin passed the winter. I believe he was snug and warm in *Iskra*'s fo'c'sle, peering out from the middle of the coiled halyards. It must have been dark in there through the long nights. Even in daytime the pale sunlight could hardly penetrate Tom's old tarpaulin cover and find a way into the fo'c'sle through the two dead-lights in *Iskra*'s sides, or through the glass light in the fo'c'sle hatch. He shared his quarters with a family of country mice, who made a nest from torn-up newspaper in the vegetable stowage on the bench opposite my Dolphin. Two of them failed to survive and I found their stiff furry bodies when I came back in the early summer. Through the winter the sea froze, the snow covered *Iskra* with a thick white eiderdown to keep her warm. The gales whined overhead, causing the forest that encircles the cove to quiver and ripple as it protected her. Tom and Toot kept watch on her, casting a friendly eye every time they had cause to venture down to the sea. Everyone in Sorrento was concerned about her as if she had been their own child.

It was a long winter for Wendy and me but a happy one as well. We got married. My business decided to pull itself together after we gave it an infusion of money, some of it book money which had built itself up in America. The business is a resilient animal. Its customers and its staff were loyal to it and came back to breathe new life into it. By the following spring it was strong enough for me to leave it again and go back for *Iskra*.

From an aeroplane the Atlantic Ocean is a large place, stretching on a clear day for hundreds of miles in all directions and containing nothing - no meaning, no physical sensation of feel and smell, no hopes, fears. The encapsulated passenger is no part of it; to him it is a coloured strip unwinding beneath him in an endless, monotonous roll, as he sits motionless far above it. He may see the outline of a ship far below but it exists in a different world from his world and he has no need or desire to comprehend it. He sees the configurations of cloud but they are flat and meaningless, having only two dimensions. Sometimes its woolly floor shuts him away from the world and he flies through his own conception of time and space, not travelling, only departing and arriving. The pilot and the engineer who manipulate the machine are his mentors, to whom he delivers his life, abrogating all decisions, all free will, all responsibility. If they do it right he steps down at his destination, raises his hat to them and goes about his business. If they do it wrong he plunges to his death with time only to fasten his belt and commend himself to his Maker. He knows that he has arrived, either in heaven or in America, but the journey, for him, has been nothing but a routine, a chore, leaving him disorientated, confused, exhausted.

From *Iskra* the ocean is a small place, full of event, sound, pleasure, danger, beauty, fear. It stretches no further than a few miles to the horizon, it teems with life and movement and variety. Each wave between America and England is encountered by *Iskra*, appraised and negotiated. Each one is different, demanding from her a different response. To the ocean sailor the sky and the clouds are part of his life, containing the ingredients of his welfare. He leaves harbour with trepidation in his soul, committing himself to the ocean with a prayer. His arrival in harbour is anticipated by days of hope and expectation which rise to fulfilment when his landfall breaks the horizon under the bowsprit. He is part of the society of living creatures which are his friends and companions. They accept him at his face value, tolerate him, even succour him although he is a trespasser in their domain. The phlegmatic ocean birds wheeling across his wake, the storm petrels bent on important business, sharks slicing the ocean with their dorsals, the small fish in tight, disciplined packs, sometimes whales, lumbering and wheezing through the ocean with benign good humour and the dolphins, creatures which are closest to him, allowing him to share in their boundless well-being.

Lucy McCabe met me from the aeroplane with my baggage full of books packed in cardboard boxes and an assortment of kitbags, grips and parcels tied with rope. I brought a new mainsail for *Iskra* made by the sailmaker in Maldon. Somehow the Customs waved on my curious assortment of baggage, too bizarre perhaps to be mischievous. Lucy took me straight to Sorrento, straight down to the foreshore where *Iskra* lay under Tom's tarpaulin. She was as I had left her. I knew from the knots on the cover which I had tied that no one had been on board. She had been left unlocked, all her gear inside her except the sails and the life raft lying in Tom's shed, my valuables scarcely more secure, in Tom's house. The house was guarded by Tom's mongrel dog, Abner, an amiable hound whose foible was to wrinkle his snout in a wistful smile and lick the hands of any intruder. All my precious possessions were intact; the incidence of crime is not high in Sorrento, East Point.

I stayed with Lucy and Jim for a couple of nights while I made *Iskra* habitable. My Dolphin was taken from his hibernation and secured back in his place, blinking in the unfamiliar light. Lucy's two daughters helped me paint the bottom with anti-fouling which Toot supplied from his store. 'Seems we run clean out of red paint 'cept for one tin,' Toot said. You can paint the other side green, then you'll always know which way you're goin'.' Tom produced a new truck that he had bought at an auction for a knock-down price. It was chained to the back of *Iskra*'s cradle. 'The Incredible Hulk', it seemed, was only used for hauling out, not launching, or perhaps its convulsions of the previous autumn had done it a mischief. There was a huge roaring and banging of exhausts and a balloon of black smoke like an atom cloud. The wheels turned, Tom sat in the cab, his foot hard on the accelerator, his body twisted round and looking back at *Iskra*. She stayed where she had been put. The wheels made six neat holes in the sand. Tom got out, pushed his hat back on his head. 'Guess she don't want to go back n'more than she wanted to come out.'

Toot was despatched for another truck and this monster was chained to the front. There was a redoubled roar. *Iskra* suddenly came with a rush and a spray of sand and pebbles from her cradle; the cavalcade set off at a brisk pace down the shore, Tom shouting and waving from the cab of the first truck, me and the girls and Jim McCabe and Joe Greene jumping up and down on the beach, smoke pouring, the whole column moving like lemmings towards the sea. Tom stopped before he drowned, Toot's truck pulled its fellow out of the sea and *Iskra* was left at the water's edge. I loaded the cradle with rocks and we waited for the tide to come in again. I buried the poor mice. They had been residents on board for the winter and deserved the dignity of a proper funeral.

Bar Harbor is six and a half miles across the bay from Sorrento. It is a resort in the high summer, sleepy and peaceful early in the year. It has a supermarket, a hardware store as only Americans know how, a fuelling dock to service the few fishermen. It was a perfect place for me to fit out *Iskra*. Sorrento, with all its charm, was impossible because it has no shops or facilities other than are offered by Tom and Toot. I have friends in Bar Harbor, Mary and Bill Drury, who offered me hospitality. I had two weeks to make

Iskra ready for the ocean and to sail 300 miles to Halifax, where Wendy would arrive on an aeroplane from England.

Iskra floated free of Tom's cradle when the tide came up, the engine started immediately, with batteries newly charged by Tom, spewing out the winter's anti-freeze from its exhaust. I motored her round to the main jetty at Sorrento where my girls loaded her spars, her steering vane and all her gear on board. Then we all set off and motored across the bay to Bar Harbor on a pale blue day in early June. Lucy came in her car and took the girls away, sadly waving as we broke the ties of friendship so newly formed. This is the sadness of cruising in foreign lands - Wendy and I suffered from it in countless places. It is a compelling reason to go back.

Bill and Mary found me a strong small boy capable of hauling me aloft and intelligent enough to pass me *Iskra*'s many halyards and stays in the right order. I scraped off the festoons of paint hanging from the cabin deck-head, lifted by the severe frost; painted round the topsides, spread gunge and paint over the cabin top in the vain hope of curing the drips, lit the fire in the cabin to air and dry her out. She was showing signs of the meagre refits and hard wear she had sustained over the past two years, she was crying out to be cared for. My Dolphin turned down his mouth; this hurried, careless care was not what he was used to. The black paint on his tail and fins was chipped, he had suffered a scrape across his cheek from a rusty mooring wire, his tail had a small piece chipped out by a random blow from an anchor fluke.

On *Iskra*'s voyage to America I saw no more of the United States than the strip of coast between Long Island and the Canadian border, with a few days' visit to San Francisco thrown in. The seething continent behind the coast, with its industries, its limitless prairies, its forests, mountains, lakes, deserts, is as much a closed book to me now as it was. The Americans we met showed us a curious mixture of compassion and aggressiveness, charm and duplicity. I came away full of half-digested impressions, conflicting experiences. A man in a motor yacht came close alongside *Iskra* as we sailed into Mystic Seaport, Connecticut, leaned over his bridge far above, shouted down, 'Say - you come over the ocean in that thing? You gotta be crazy.' Then he turned the stern of his boat to us, with its twin exhaust orifices like muttering fumeroles, let in the throttle and enveloped *Iskra* in a cloud of sulphurous black smoke. A girl in her twenties we saw in the ice cream parlour in Newport was so obese that her arms stuck out from her body like a teddy bear's arms, stiff and straight; her feet, protruding from underneath the cone shape of her body, waddled her across to a mechanical cream dispenser which she used to spread a thick layer of chocolate over an immense ice cream she then began to lick and swallow. She was worshipping plenty, offering herself as a sacrifice to the god of consumption. Obesity, we noted, is the most obvious American disease. Conversely, fitness is another religion. A couple who are friends of Wendy's, whom she stayed with when she was in Texas, would get up early in the morning and jog round a suburb of Dallas for at least an hour every day. They would then take Wendy out to breakfast at the drug store - pancakes covered in maple syrup, sausage, bacon, egg, tomatoes, on one huge plate. We met an old sea captain in Ile au Haut who deposited fresh vegetables on *Iskra*'s deck before we were awake each morning. The local postmaster was an ex-stockbroker who had thrown up New York for the simple life. We met people who lived on an island in Maine, had built their house out of the forest, fished and planted the land for a living. We met people who were kind to us, would put themselves to endless trouble for our convenience. We did our modest business with Nunk Allen and Tom and Toot who were as straight as oak planks. The publisher of *Schooner Integrity*, in Boston, reneged on my royalties.

I set out in good time from Bar Harbor to meet Wendy in Halifax - in too much haste, remembering last year's trauma in the fog. To come back to *Iskra* after an absence of nearly eight months and then to set off straight into the ocean was a stupidity. I ought to have given myself at least a few days to finish fitting out properly, to see that all the gear was working correctly and to spend some time sailing round the coast to acclimatise myself again to the business of sailing alone. It takes time for the mind and the body to be tuned to solitude, to get back into a sea-going sleep routine, to be physically strong again after the debilitating sloth of life ashore. In going straight to sea I neglected one of the cardinal rules I have made for myself.

At first it was calm and foggy when I set out from Bar Harbor for Cape Sable on the southern tip of Nova Scotia, a notorious graveyard for ships with swirling, unpredictable currents, fickle winds off the sheer cliffs and frequent fog. By the time I came up with the Cape I was already tired; I hadn't slept the previous night.

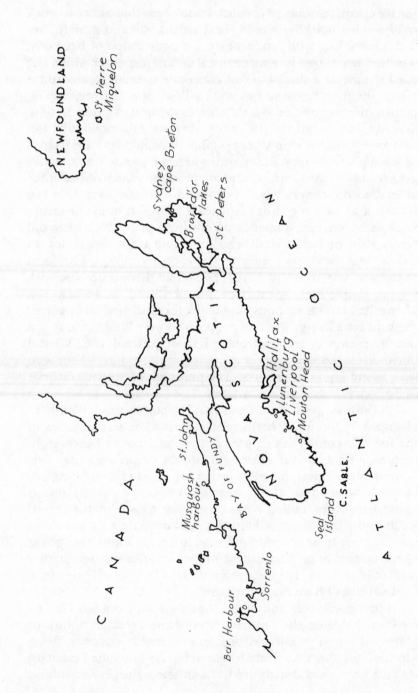

As the light faded I heard a strange swishing noise all around. At first it made no sense. It sounded like the bow waves of a dozen fast-moving ships, or a dozen gliding aeroplanes, or heavy rain in a forest. A spout of water leapt up within feet of *Iskra*, and a black body slid past her side. They were all around, blowing and sucking, the heaving shapes barnacled and mottled with weed. I could see their blowholes and the great horizontal tail fins breaking the surface as they sounded - any one of them powerful enough to smash *Iskra* to matchwood with a single careless flick. I ran to the foredeck in alarm, looked around the tight perimeter of fog. A dozen black shapes rolled and tumbled past *Iskra*; the air was full of condensed sea blown upward and falling like dew, there was the hiss of giants' breath. 'Be careful, whales,' I shouted. I appealed to my Dolphin. 'Tell your big cousins to take care.' They heard me and went on their way, leaving the air vibrating with their blowing.

I went to sleep, taking a bearing on Seal Island which I could now see, steadying *Iskra* on what seemed a safe course to clear the Cape and setting my alarm for an hour ahead. It was a night of fickle breezes, thickening fog and rogue currents in which *Iskra* was taken in all directions. I slept through the alarm, through all my in-built mechanisms; when morning came she had lost herself. Now I could hear nothing and see nothing. The wind was freshening from the south-west and the barometer was tumbling. She needed reefing and the jib changing. I thought she was clear of the Cape and had eased the sheet and set course to take her up the Nova Scotia coast, congratulating myself on my good luck to have slept in such a place and still be alive, when I heard, loud and clear and from above, the booming of a lighthouse on *Iskra*'s starboard bow. Why had I not heard it before? Was it a freak of the fog or of my own fatigue, or had Cape Sable really been silent, or its sound carried away from me by the freshening wind? We had been set inshore, just as the sailing directions warn, but more quickly and farther than I would have believed possible. By hauling the sheet and pinching her into a rising head sea, I was able to claw her to windward of the Cape. The lighthouse boomed above my head, invisible but close - too close. We sailed within yards of the off-lying rocks; I saw them like decaying teeth, through the fog.

I gave *Iskra* an extra point to seaward of her course up the coast. It wasn't enough to save me from another fright. Off Mouton

Head, halfway to Lunenburg, she was set in again so that I found myself inside a group of dangerous offshore rocks, broken water appearing suddenly to seaward. We gained clear water again only after another frightening few minutes. I found myself destroyed by this last mischance, shaking and mouthing a prayer as *Iskra* beat to seaward again. The Pilot talks of magnetic anomalies; more likely it was carelessness, a rebuke for going straight to sea from a winter's idleness.

The wind showed no sign of moderating. Demoralized and scared, I decided to take *Iskra* into Liverpool, a few miles short of Lunenburg, an easy entrance marked by a radio beacon. Here I waited at anchor in the lee of the forested shore until the weather moderated and I regained my nerve and composure. Then *Iskra* sailed round to Lunenburg on a beautiful, clear sunlit day and entered this most protected and friendly of all harbours.

In Lunenburg there were no problems, only friendliness. It is still one of the world's seagoing towns, anyone arriving from the ocean is assured of help and kindness. Pat Fry, who herself sailed from the east coast of England with her daughter Zoë as part of the crew, made sure *Iskra* had every need fulfilled. She loaned her old car so that Wendy could be fetched by road from Halifax. I drove it up the long, straight empty road through the forest of Nova Scotia, waited in anxiety until I saw the aeroplane roll up in front of the airport building and her trim form step down. The meetings are joyous, the partings ever more harrowing.

Wendy had more books in her luggage. We found Lunenburg a good town for an itinerant vendor of nautical books - it breathes salt water. The old houses of the original Grand Banks schooner owners are still there, all in gaily painted clapboard with filigree round the doors and windows, and extravagant cupolas from where the fishermen's wives watched the sea for the return of their husbands from the banks. The church might have come from the top of a German Christmas cake. The yard that built the schooner *Bluenose* in 1921, and her successor *Bluenose II* in 1963, still built wooden boats if it could get the orders. The foreman, Klein Faulkenheim, was the son of the yard foreman who built the original *Bluenose*. The place still reeked of sail. Arthur Dauphinee still made wooden blocks and spars; his name was a byword to every restorer of wooden boats, he sent his blocks all over the world. He was a man full of quiet humour and kindness.

We stayed in Lunenburg for longer than we had intended because the place was so friendly and delightful. We had the use of Pat Fry's old motor car and she and her friends made a great fuss of us. We loved the emptiness of Nova Scotia, the feeling of space and freedom, the enthusiasm for everything connected with the sea. Our limited supply of books soon began to melt away. We gave *Iskra* a new set of main sheet blocks on a barter deal - blocks for books - with Arthur Dauphinee, took our friends for a sail in the bay and left for Halifax.

The eastern seaboard of Nova Scotia is an uncomfortable place for a yacht; a heavy swell from the ocean is always present, often agitated by currents and overlaid by rough seas from sudden strong winds. The day we left Lunenburg the wind failed us and *Iskra* rolled dementedly, her gear flogging from side to side, the heavy boom banging up against the sheet with sickening force, the gaff swinging across as she rolled, just as it had done in the Gulf Stream. Wendy was seasick, she spewed her heart into a bucket. Nothing I could do would give her relief. I tried *Iskra* on different courses, I tried running the engine, I tried every ruse I could think of to keep the boat still and bring her a measure of comfort. She was a picture of profound misery. Wendy had never been on an ocean passage on board *Iskra*, not because of her seasickness but because she had never been able to leave her job for long enough. She had never been exposed to the uneven, quick motion of a yacht at sea for long enough for her body to accustom itself, therefore she believed that she would go on being sick for ever. While I was below ministering to her needs in the night, offering her all manner of palliatives - dry biscuits, drinks of water, pills, advice, all given with the patronising tolerance of the person who has never suffered from the ailment, there was a sudden noise from aloft, a cracking, splintering, tearing noise. I dropped the bucket beside her and ran out - *Iskra*'s gaff was broken in half. 'Come on - quick - sail's got to come down.'

I ran for'ard to the halyards. In the moonlight I could see the broken gaff hanging drunkenly, its jagged end held by the sail - the sail would tear in minutes. Wendy came up at once, helping to gather in the sail, finding the tyers and securing it as it came down, hauling in the sheet until the boom was bowsed down on the gallows, seasickness forgotten. We had a brief look at the gaff, broken clean in half; I noticed there was an old fracture there which I had never seen under the layers of varnish. 'We'll have to set the storm trysail - it's all we can do until we get in to Halifax.' She ran below to the fo'c'sle, came up with the sail and we set it together. Enough breeze came to fill the trysail and steady *Iskra* on course; there were lights to be distinguished and to mark on the chart. We set about unrigging the gaff from the sail, the new mainsail had held together and was undamaged. At dawn we came up with the approach to Halifax harbour, turned to port and were soon in sheltered water.

The broken gaff was a disguised blessing. Because we were in trouble everyone flocked to help us. Dave and Ruth Wood whose boat we berthed alongside rallied to our support. Ruth fed us while we worked on the gaff, Dave produced all manner of tools and materials and advice. People came from all around to assist. We were entertained, taken off in motor cars to see the Province of Nova Scotia and made a huge fuss of. A workshop was set up on the dock and the gaff was ceremoniously joined together, glued, through-bolted and fibreglassed. It looked a strong job. Wiseacres from all over Halifax pronounced it a workmanlike repair. My Dolphin was more sceptical. He had no wish to be committed to the ocean with a broken gaff, repaired by a bunch of amateurs on Halifax quay.

When we left, with much waving and good wishes, *Iskra* set off into the ocean in a smart breeze. At first all was well - she tramped out of the harbour in fine style. Off Devil's Island the wind fell light and then to a calm. Once again she was helpless in the swell, the gear crashing from side to side. Once again Wendy's rosy complexion turned to pale puce, her eyes glazed, her expression soured, her spirits plummeted. I was casting about in my mind for some occupation for her of overriding urgency when there was another and familiar crack from up the mast. I looked aloft in time to see the gaff fold over on itself and commence to dig holes in the sail with its jagged end. 'Quick - it's happened again. All hands on deck - that means you.' Together we struggled to get the sail down and to bring the broken gaff to the deck where it could do no harm. *Iskra* limped back to Halifax.

We held counsel with Dave and Ruth and half a dozen friends - the outcome was Lunenburg. 'That's the only place you'll get a new gaff made quickly,' Dave said. 'Take my car, drive to Lunenburg, and get Arthur Dauphinee to make you one. Make him do it tomorrow - I'll need the car on Saturday without fail.' Dave's car was about the size of our flat in London, with automatic drive and an alarming array of instruments, levers, flashing lights, buzzes, pings. I perched behind the wheel, Wendy beside me clutching a map, the broken pieces of the gaff stowed away in the boot which was the size of a small cargo hold. We jerked and bounced our way out of Halifax and on to the highway to Lunenburg, sixty miles to the west. Canadian drivers are more patient, courteous and in less of a hurry than their English counterparts; no one swore at us. We arrived in Lunenburg late, knocked up a sleepy Pat Fry for a bed, were outside Arthur's factory at breakfast time. When he saw the spar he said, 'I'd sure like to help you good people but my lathes are too small - there's nothing I can do, I guess.' Arthur began to telephone his friends and business people he knew but drew no luck. 'There's a guy can do it in two weeks,' he said. The hours ticked away. We began to lose hope.

Disheartened we wandered along the quay towards the Ship Museum; I had sold them books, perhaps they could suggest something. We ran into Captain Mitchell on the dock. 'We need the spar today,' we said to him hopelessly. 'Damn it,' he said, 'there's a shipyard in this town crying out for work - sure they'll do it for you.' Captain Mitchell bundled us and the broken gaff into his car, drove us along to the yard and took us to Klein Faulkenheim, a mild, quiet man with a humorous light in his eye. 'Yeah, I guess we can do it - in a week.' He glanced at us. 'Well, maybe a couple of days.' He looked at Wendy's face, her mouth turned down. 'Well, maybe I can rough something out today - but you'll have to finish it, put on the ironwork, sand it down and all that.'

He started straight away, taking on the job himself with one of the yard shipwrights to help him. They shaped the new spar from a baulk of Douglas fir, seasoned in the yard and ready. 'The *Bluenose*'s spars were made of the same wood.' he said. They worked quickly, silently, and with the smooth, oiled precision of craftsmen. The spar was finished by 3 pm; not roughed out but finished - planed, sanded, coated with Cuprinol and the ironwork fitted. We drove back to Halifax with it lashed to the side of Dave's Cadillac. A cheer went up as we arrived alongside *Iskra*. She was at sea again the next morning.

The days turned themselves into weeks as we sailed up the Nova Scotia coast. We had the same experience as the year before; I had intended to cruise to Newfoundland, to St Pierre Michelon, to Despair Bay, before setting off across the ocean for home but it was all too wonderful to hurry. I began to dread when my crew would go, as go she must. We never felt like strangers in Nova Scotia, there was an easy friendliness, a relaxed acceptance of a yacht cruising from England. Canada is refreshing, there is a feeling of space, the pace of life is less hurried, people will pass the time of day,there is the interest to ask questions, the frankness to answer them. There is an endearing, slow humour about the place.

The size of Canada in relation to the number of people is awe inspiring. In the Bras d'Or Lakes we went for a walk one evening from an anchorage in a place called Little Harbour. It was huge - a basin a mile across, the forest down to the beach, entrance through a cut twenty yards wide, no vessel to be seen except *Iskra*. We found a road through the forest and set off hoping to come across a shop, even a pub or a hotel with a bar. After four miles we had seen no sign of any human life. In another mile a car came along with a man and a woman in it. They were astonished to find us walking, a most unusual activity. They took us to a farm on a hill overlooking a stretch of island-dotted azure water - beaches, woods, sheltered inlets, all empty. Another house two miles further on was built on a promontory overlooking the sea. The man had built it himself, hewing wood from the forest, sinking his own well, generating his own electricity with the wind. He needed no planning permission, no truck with building regulations. 'I worked in Ontario; one day I said 'to Hell' and came here.' Wendy and I thought we might say 'to Hell' one day.

For 200 miles north-east of Halifax the coast is indented with dozens of inlets and anchorages and harbours, many of them with off-lying dangers but all well marked. Owls Head Bay, Ship Harbour, Chezzetcook Inlet, Liscombe Mills and then St Peter's where the Bras d'Or Lakes are entered through a lock. Here there are hundreds of miles of sheltered sailing in fresh water, free of fog. We met Farley Mowat, one of Canada's most honoured writers in a country that respects writers. We sailed through the lakes, far away from jobs and business and banks and politicians and newspapers, through a dream world of calm waters, trees, happiness. Canadians are sympathetic towards the English; we found them gentler, more restrained than Americans.

In Canada as in America we saw no slums, no industrial wastelands, no black ghettos. From our point of vantage in the serene backwaters of Nova Scotia and Maine it was hard to believe that such things exist, hard to believe that there is a word spelled 'poverty'. We had to pinch ourselves, remind ourselves of begging children in Puerto Rico, of the shanty towns in Jamaica, of the black suburb of Dallas, Texas, where Wendy worked as a nurse. In a world where two-thirds are next door to starvation, where 700 million souls live in absolute poverty, Wendy and I are among a privileged minority who have enough - we are even a minority of a minority.

Wendy left from Sydney, Cape Breton, at the northeastern tip of Nova Scotia. We went to the airport in a taxi, clutching hands silently. I couldn't tell her that I was frightened, that I would take any excuse to abandon this last voyage. I couldn't tell her because I knew she was frightened, for me and for herself. I could tell no one because to admit fright is unacceptable; the precept was hammered into my head as a child that I could never admit to being afraid. I have carried the burden through my life, now I haven't the courage to be a coward. 'You must be lonely out there.' they say. 'No, no - I like solitude.' 'But isn't it frightening in a storm, alone in the ocean?' 'No, no - I'm used to it.' It was true once, now it's a lie. I am frightened until I pray to a deity I did not think I believed in, lonely until my being aches for a word of sympathy. When the day comes and my hand is on the anchor cable it is too late. I am not brave enough to call it off.

I watched her go from behind the airport fence, my fingers hooked through the mesh like a prisoner watching the departure of his visitor. Her form grew smaller as she walked out to the aeroplane, one of a motley knot thrown together by chance, her identity lost. I saw her turn on the steps, look back confusedly, wave, disappear. Could she have gone for ever? I felt the tears well up from somewhere deep inside. They poured down my cheeks, I felt my face twist, I felt my body heave and shudder. I saw the aeroplane turn and roll away, heard its roar, watched as it rose up through the secret cloud. As my tears poured it flew off into an inexplicable future.

I walked back the four miles to *Iskra*, the salt water rolling down my face, caught in a trap I had laid for myself. Through two summers this moment had come closer day by day. I had turned it over in my mind, considered it in the wakeful hours of the night, reasoned it through. 'If I have done it before, surely I can do it again? Solitude? I love it, thrive on it, am happy with it. *Iskra* is strong, the ocean can't harm her - she'll come through as she has always come through.' But it is all different now, life has become valuable - to me and to Wendy. 'Be careful,' she says to me, 'Please, please be careful.' All right, I'll be careful.

Sometimes we judge ourselves by what others think of us; burying the truth under the layers of bravado we mistake the front for our real selves. As I made my way back to *Iskra* I understood that I had fallen into this trap. Now I had no wish to risk my skin. I had found my happiness, it was up there in bright sunshine above the sultry cloud that covered the bay of Sydney, Cape Breton. I wanted to keep it, have it beside me, not gamble it in a last, senseless throw that could lose me all and gain me nothing. Like a drowning man the whole compass of my experience flashed across my mind as I strode through the streets towards where *Iskra* lay at anchor, small and fragile and infinitely vulnerable. It was no great act of will that had brought me to the beginning of this voyage, no clear cut, deliberate choice; rather it was a long accumulation of small acts and decisions, of no consequence in themselves but, taken together, building themselves into this actuality which I could not escape from. It is the small choices that shape the course of our lives; the big decisions, when they come, are forced on us and made inevitable by what has gone before.

I bought the last of my stores in the supermarket by the quay, mechanically ticking them off the list that Wendy and I had made the day before, filled *Iskra*'s tanks with water and diesel, gave the last coins in my pocket to a small boy who looked at me with pleased surprise, rowed on board, deflated and stowed my rubber dinghy and hauled on the anchor chain. It came up over the bow with the measured, rhythmic clank which is and has always been the music of a ship going to sea. The sound imparted to me a measure of confidence.

If I needed excuse or encouragement to swallow the single-handed anchor, *Iskra*'s voyage from Sydney, Cape Breton to Falmouth would have provided it. My journal says of July 27th: 'It's blowing hard - Force 8 or more. The dawn is a waste of grey and white heaving up and down like a huge eiderdown with the top ripped off. It is frightening when I think how far I am from any other person - a thousand miles from land on all sides. I don't think about that too much. *Iskra* gives off a great feeling of security and safety, but sometimes I think she is very frail.

Sometimes I think there's not much that can harm her with her storm trysail and reefed staysail unless she hits some freak piece of bad luck.'

On July 30th: 'Will there ever be a nice day? The aftermath of a gale is very beautiful. First a break in the clouds and a tiny patch of blue, a Dutchman's Trousers they call it. Then the clouds begin to break - some almost black, some snowy white and the sun comes through and turns the grey sea to vivid blue. The breaking waves stand out like neon lights, winking on and off over the whole seascape. Very slowly the whine of the wind slackens and the boat, suddenly relieved of pressure is hurled about like a toy boat in a bath. Now the seas slop on board, sometimes heavily, tumbling down on top of the cabin and shutting out the light, but they no longer have the venom which drove them at the height of the gale. I hope this will ease tonight; my Dolphin is tired of it - so am I. My fear is that it will go to the east which would stop progress. Already she's as close to the wind as she will go with storm sails. This is a bleak place I'm in. I wonder what I can be doing out here? I looked for some comfort, some sign of better things to come in the sunset, but found none. It was all yellow shafts with no hint of a softer pink, and when the sun broke through just before dusk it was like a lump of soft putty, all puce and festering. No hope for tomorrow from that quarter.'

On August 3rd: 'As I was getting the mainsail in the wind came screaming down - a fierce gust, the precursor of what is to come. Got the trysail up and snugged down as best I could and left her to it. It got steadily worse as the daylight came and now it's blowing harder than Force 8. Is this number four? I've lost count. Everything's wet again, drips all going full belt, seas breaking on deck, mist and blown spume outside and the unending grey waves with their white tops. Sometimes there's a real crash but mostly she finds her way through. I'll be pleased when it stops, then perhaps we'll get something a bit decent to finish the voyage with.'

'She's never stopped moving towards home. The seas have been crashing down on her from above with sickening force. Just now one hit so hard I thought the cabin top had broken open. Water swilling about over the floor which I can't get out except with the electric pump - and I've no more battery. It isn't much but it's horrible. She gets hit by seas so hard and so suddenly that it frightens the life out of me. I've only once been in a worse gale than this. I haven't had sleep since the night before last. I took in the trysail tomake her safer, reefed the staysail. Working on deck is amazing. I hang on for my life. One of the hanks came off the staysail - I had to go right into the bows to put it on again. I made tea with great difficulty - then spilt boiling water on my hand and knocked over the teapot. Swore uncontrollably. This is not my day. I would like this gale to stop before it does me a mischief.'

'Writing all this down is good therapy. I went up and reefed the trysail and set it again and she is much better. Then the wind eased quite suddenly. The sky's awful and there's a huge swell so that I have to move about with extreme care both inside and out for fear of hurting myself or being hurled overboard.'

On Friday August 6th: 'This passage is ending in the manner in which it has proceeded. If nothing busts and the wind doesn't head any more I will get into Falmouth sometime tomorrow. But this is not going to be a nice afternoon. She's pushing into a very big sea in a very strong wind, spray over all the time and sometimes the sea comes rolling over the cabin top like a green animal with white teeth. As she got closer to the land the sea went down and she began to sail fast. Still a lot of wind - the radio beacon on the Lizard is right ahead. At 18.10 I woke after a short sleep and saw the land - England! Very misty and thick but no doubt of it - England, beautiful, beautiful England. I have done no washing since I left America - there hasn't been a day when I could have dried it. They'll put me in a decontamination centre when I get to Falmouth.'

I made one more single-handed voyage after *Iskra* came home from America - I took her to Iceland. Wendy and I sailed her round the north of the island, from Reykjavik round the northern capes and fjords to Akureyri. On Midsummer's Day in 1985 we stood side by side, with no other soul within miles, on the massive promontory of Straumnes, with the capes of the northern fjords we had already sailed past standing out in the ocean to the west; Iceland's Cape Horn, still to be rounded, close to the eastward of us. *Iskra* was a tiny dot anchored in Adalvik Bay far below us. We watched the midnight sun dip to the horizon, roll along it like a fiery football and slowly rise again into the pale sky.

We suffered another agonising parting at Akureyri when Wendy's time came to go home, this one, we swore, our last. I sailed *Iskra* back to Bradwell on my last lone voyage. I nearly lost her within four miles of Bradwell creek. Through fatigue and the misjudgements a man commits when he is fatigued I put her ashore on Colne Point on a wild night. It was a freak of fortune that got her off undamaged, a chance I swore I would never take again. I have had my share of good fortune - I mean to save it, not waste it on any more single-handed capers. From now on, Wendy and I are in this business together or not at all.

Now *Iskra* is back in her winter quarters, with her bow to the sailmaker's grassy quay in Maldon, Essex. My Dolphin peers round at the piles of wood, the upturned dinghy, the old steam tug which lies alongside, the settled tranquility of the place. He passes the time of day with his old friend the rat, mulling over his adventures, unburdening his collected wisdom, wondering what the future holds for him. Wendy and I live close by now, no more than a short walk along the Downs Road. When the winter gales scream overhead we can keep an eye on my Dolphin, make sure he is at all times securely fast, make sure he is provided for and looked after as he should be. Soon we shall both want him again for a new venture, together this time, perhaps, to Argentina to visit my cousins?

She lies with her bow to the quay outside the sailmaker's loft